Fantastic Painted Finishes

Fantastic Pa

TWENTY-EIGHT RECIPES

FOR TRANSFORMING

ORDINARY OBJECTS INTO

EXTRAORDINARY

TREASURES

inted Finishes

Lisa Wassong *with* Steven Schwartz

Photographs *by* Richard Lovrich

A Stepping Stone Book
Crown Trade Paperbacks
New York

For my mother, who opened the door, and for Joseph Arkus, who pushed me through it.
Lisa

For Elisabeth, who can be whatever she makes up her mind to be.
Steve

Photographs on pages 17, 21, 23, 35, 87, 100 courtesy of Beth Phillips

Copyright © 1994 by Lisa Wassong with Steven Schwartz

Published by Crown Publishers, Inc., 201 East 50th Street, New York, New York 10022. Member of the Crown Publishing Group.
Random House, Inc. New York, Toronto, London, Sydney, Auckland

CROWN TRADE PAPERBACKS and colophon are trademarks of Crown Publishers, Inc.

Manufactured in Hong Kong

Design by Kay Schuckhart

Library of Congress Cataloging-in-Publication Data
Wassong, Lisa
Fantastic Painted Finishes: 28 Recipes for Transforming Ordinary Objects into Extraordinary Treasures / Lisa Wassong with Steven Schwartz. —
1st ed.
p. cm.
1. Painting—Technique. 2. Decoration and ornament.
I. Schwartz, Steven A. II. Title.
TT385.W38 1994
745.7—dc20 93-26460
CIP

ISBN 0-517-88176-4

10 9 8 7 6 5 4 3 2 1
First Edition

CONTENTS

ACKNOWLEDGMENTS

We would like to thank Sarah Jane Freymann—sister, wife, agent—who thought of this book in the first place . . . Dominique Lange—friend and colleague—who was there every step of the way . . . and Erica Marcus—editor extraordinaire—who provided vision, support, and the book's fabulous title.

INTRODUCTION

It seems as if I've *always* been interested in painted finishes. My family spent summers traveling through Europe when I was a child, and I saw painted finishes almost everywhere—in beautiful Italian churches, gracious French homes, and glorious Spanish castles. All these places seemed to glow with decorated walls, floors, doors, furniture, and objets d'art. As I moved through careers as a ballet dancer, fashion buyer, and interior designer, this interest moved with me. And when I finally took a class in *creating* painted finishes, I knew I'd found what I wanted to do.

Since the mid-1970s, I have studied, taught, designed, and produced painted finishes. And to me, there is nothing more exciting or satisfying than introducing people to this world of color, beauty, shape, form, and fantastic possibilities.

Painted finishes are appealing as an outlet for anyone's artistic impulses. Just because you can't sketch, draw, sculpt, knit, crochet, weave, carve, quilt, make pottery, or paint (even by the numbers) doesn't mean you can't create extraordinary finishes.

Creating painted finishes teaches you about yourself: You learn where you have patience and where you don't, what's fun and what isn't, where you're gifted and where you're *more* gifted. And then, you change. What seemed hard becomes easier, what seemed intimidating becomes challenging, and

what seemed boring becomes interesting. I've seen this happen time and time again.

There's no doubt that painted finishes are "magic." I don't know any other word for them. And sometimes the magic is in the process—and sometimes the magic's in you.

For example, crumple a piece of plastic wrap, dab it over a wet green-painted surface, and—*presto chango*—before your eyes is spinach malachite, a finish that depends solely on your ability to follow instructions.

On the other hand, *gem* malachite is much more than dabbing paint with plastic wrap—*it's* magic depends on shapes and designs drawn by *you*. A beautiful result here is the outcome of imagination, creativity, and skill.

I have chosen the specific finish for each object in this book for one of two reasons: either because I know how great it will look, or because I'm familiar with the decor a particular piece must work with. As far as you're concerned, however, consider these choices as a guide; feel free to experiment with any finish you like, on any object you want. After a while, you will develop a personal aesthetic about what goes best with what—but at the beginning, do whatever appeals to you. My credo for this book is "Fast, fun, and practical," so even if this is your very first try, you will achieve results quickly . . . have a good time doing it . . . and wind up with a fantastic piece.

Painted finishes have been used throughout history to decorate objects and beautify environments. And in this regard, we're no different from our ancestors. The earliest ones decorated their caves with colors that came from the earth, and we decorate our "caves" as well—with the very same earth tones they used. In the same way, when we can't afford marble, we create it. When there's no lapis, we simulate it. When the wood is poor quality, we beautify it.

And, as we continue to become more ecology-conscious, more and more protective of our planet's natural resources, painted finishes provide a wonderful way to decorate without using up, wasting, or throwing away anything.

My approach to teaching painted finishes is *step by step* and *little by little.* And having said that, I'm reminded of the time I took a skiing lesson in Vermont. It was a freezing cold day and we were at the very top of a mountain. All I saw when I looked down was a sheet of ice. Although I could ski pretty well, I was frightened. "I can't go down that whole sheet of ice," I said to the instructor. "Of course you can't," she replied, "but you can go the first foot." What was true about getting down a mountain in Vermont is also true about painted finishes. The only way to go from an ugly "before" to a stunning "after" is *one step at a time.*

In all my years of teaching, I've never been able to tell in advance what someone will find easy or difficult. Therefore, I haven't ranked the projects in the book in any order of difficulty. For the same reason, I've generalized about the time needed to accomplish each step. For example, if I allot an hour for leafing and you finish in forty-five minutes, it probably means you're good at leafing, not that you've done anything wrong.

Even though the project instructions here (I call them recipes) are pretty self-contained, I haven't repeated everything I have to say about materials, color, preparation, varnishing, and cleanup in every one of them, so please read all the introductory sections before you begin working. If you don't, you won't find out how to use a lazy Susan, what "Saral paper" is, what to do if you choose the "wrong" color, why 20 coats of varnish provide less protection than 6 coats, and why you should be careful where you put down a paintbrush when the phone rings.

Where to begin? How to begin? Well, just leaf through the book until something catches your eye—a finish, a color, an object. Look through the At a Glance section to get a sense of the steps involved, then read through the Materials and Step by Step sections. If this is your first try, the only other advice I can give is to pick an object that doesn't strike you as being very complicated or time-consuming. *One step at a time* helps ease you into the fascinating world of painted finishes.

1

BEFORE YOU START

MATERIALS

*a*LMOST EVERYTHING YOU NEED FOR THE RECIPES IN THIS BOOK CAN BE FOUND AT YOUR LOCAL HARDWARE, PAINT, OR ARTIST'S SUPPLY STORE. THESE THREE SOURCES WILL EITHER STOCK WHAT YOU WANT ALREADY, BE ABLE TO GET IT FOR YOU, OR TELL YOU WHERE YOU CAN FIND IT. YOU CAN ALSO CHECK IN A SEARS, ONE OF THE SUPER-CHAIN DRUGSTORES, AND EVEN IN A FIVE-AND-TEN. JUST TO BE SURE, HOWEVER, I'VE INCLUDED A SOURCE LIST (WITH ADDRESSES AND PHONE NUMBERS) AT THE END OF THE BOOK. IF YOU ABSOLUTELY STRIKE OUT WHERE YOU LIVE, YOU MIGHT TRY ONE OF THESE. (START WITH JANOVIC

Plaza. They have a catalog available and do a large mail-order business). What follows is an alphabetical list of the materials used in the book. I've included only the information I think is useful (or interesting), but if you want to know more, just ask someone where you do your buying.

I always tend to use national-brand products whenever possible. These companies have a reputation to protect, so you can usually be assured of consistent quality. I'm going to mention these brands as I go along, and you might want to try them if they're available to you. A note of caution, however: Environmental concerns are causing great changes in the paint industry. I think this is terrific and long overdue. But these changes affect the character of latex paint, oil paint, glazecoat, and varnish. All the major companies are looking for the best balance of price, quality, and safety, and for the foreseeable future this might affect drying time and sheen. Please be aware of this as you work.

ALCOHOL We always use "denatured" alcohol in painted finishes. This product can be bought in *any* paint or hardware store and is used to clean the piece we're working on, to thin or dilute shellac, to clean brushes we've used to apply shellac, and to clean dried acrylic or latex paint.

ARCHITECT'S TAPE This comes in various colors and various sizes (from ⅟₃₂″ to ¼″). It's made of matte or shiny plastic and is used by architects to create and/or enhance their designs. It serves the same design and decoration function for us and is typically available in artist's supply stores.

BOLE In gilding, different color clay—called bole—is used as a base. Red clay brings out the brilliance of gold leaf, blue clay brings out the brilliance of silver leaf, and yellow clay simulates gold in areas where craftspeople don't want to waste the real thing (like on the back of a table or chest, or the underside of chairs and drawers). Even though we don't gild or leaf like this in *Fantastic Painted*

Finishes, we still use the word to refer to the colors of paint used under the different kinds of leaf.

BONDING LIQUID When you're not sure a surface (like Formica or plastic) will accept paint, you apply a coat of a cleaning and bonding liquid like Wil-Bond. Unfortunately, this product has an unpleasant smell.

BRONZE POWDERS These are more accurately called "metallic" powders and are made of various materials: copper, aluminum, silver, plus different golds— from bright and extrabright to green-gold. Bronze powders are used to add sparkle to a finish, or to simulate gold leaf (mix with a little shellac or varnish and you have a pretty terrific gold paint). Bronze powders can be bought in artist's supply stores, or wherever leaf is sold.

BRUSHES Made of various materials, they come in different shapes and sizes.

Poly brushes are made of foam, are available in 1″ to 4″ widths, are very inexpensive, and are used when working on flat or semiflat surfaces. If you use poly brushes with water-base paint or water-base varnish, you can wash them out (in water) and use them again. After use with oil- or alcohol-based products, however, throw poly brushes away. The alcohol or mineral spirits needed to clean them actually cost more than buying new brushes.

Use poly brushes when you're still figuring out if painted finishes are going to be an occasional or a serious hobby. You can buy them in any hardware store.

Synthetic brushes can be bought in hardware or artist's supply stores and are used with acrylic, latex, and oil paints. They come in flat and round shapes and a complete range of sizes. The brands I like in synthetic brushes—and in the natural brushes that follow—are Grumbacher and Windsor & Newton.

Natural brushes are used with oil-based paint and oil-based

varnish and should **not** be used with water-based products (the plastic in the synthetics ruins them—they go soft and limp and become basically useless). There are many kinds of natural brushes:

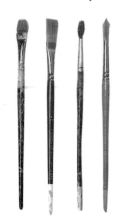

Oxhair is used with oil varnish because the soft, smooth, long hair doesn't leave brush marks. These brushes are best on flat (or relatively flat) surfaces. They can be purchased in artist's supply stores.

Bristle is used for pouncing and spattering, when a brush with body is needed. Bristle brushes can be bought in hardware and paint stores. *Artist* bristle brushes (which can only be bought in artist's supply stores) are used for fine detail work.

Sable is used in artist brushes because it's very soft, holds paint well, and responds to the movement of your hand (as when you're making a design that swoops and swirls). Sable brushes can be bought in artist's supply stores. They are expensive and must be taken care of.

Badger is used for blending because it's long-haired and very soft. Badger is extremely expensive (cosmetic and shaving brushes are made of it), so badger brushes should be purchased only when you've become relatively serious about painted finishes. An artist's supply store carries badger brushes.

Rabbit is also very soft and can be used to blend or varnish. Although rabbit is very inexpensive, it doesn't hold up. A rabbit brush loses its hair quickly, then must be thrown out. These brushes are so cheap, however, that it's economically sensible to use them when starting out. Hardware and paint stores are the source for rabbit brushes.

A Few Tips:

• If you're a beginner, buy brushes only as you need them. As you move from project to project, you will acquire all the variety you need. Don't rush out and buy a great deal of expensive materi-als until you're sure you're going to use them. I can't tell you how many brushes and how much paint I've inherited over the years from enthusiastic beginners who spent a small fortune before realizing that for them, painted finishes were a casual flirtation rather than a long-term love affair. Never spend money needlessly.

• If you're a little more advanced than a beginner, you probably have some of these brushes already—or close enough to them. I mean, if I specify a 2" badger and you already have a 1½", obviously it will work just fine.

• Never use brushes to mix paint. It will ruin them. The only exception is mixing artist oils with a small, stiff artist bristle brush.

• To find out about cleaning brushes, please refer to the Cleanup section on page 23.

BUTCHER'S WAX This is actually floor wax and can be bought in any hardware or paint store. It is high in turpentine, mixes well with dry pigments, and is usually made from fine bee's wax. In this book we mix butcher's wax with rotten stone (ground pumice) for antiquing (see Recipe 4 on page 41, a Statue of Buddha.)

DRY PIGMENTS When elements like rock, clay, earth, and coal are ground into a powder they are called "dry pigments." They must be mixed with a medium of some sort (in this book we use wax and vinegar), and are used when we want to make our own colors. Artist's supply stores will be your source for dry pigments and almost all of them carry the basic earth tones (raw umber, burnt umber, raw sienna, burnt sienna, black, and French yellow ochre). Whatever they don't carry, they can order for you.

FILLER fills holes, gouges, and deep scratches in whatever material you're working with—from wood and plastic to metal and even plaster. You can buy filler in any hardware store but be sure to read the label instructions—drying times can vary from brand to brand.

GLAZE is a thin layer of transparent color spread over a painted surface. In the book we use two kinds of glaze: oil-base (which is oil paint, glaze-coat, and mineral spirits) and water-base (water-based paint, acrylic varnish, and water). After a glaze is applied, we manipulate it in some way, and depending on how, we get wood, marble, stone, mineral, or a design. In painted finishes, *everything* is one of only two procedures: We either put glaze on and leave it on, or put glaze on and partially remove it.

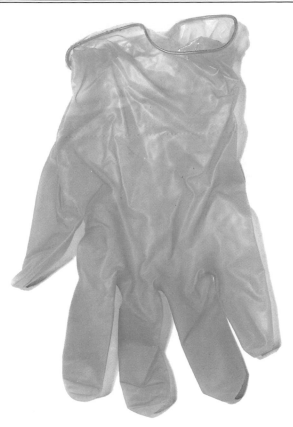

GLAZECOAT is a liquid treatment used to give body and transparency to glaze. It can be purchased in paint or hardware stores. In this book, we use glazecoat with oil-based paints only. I like the McCloskey brand, Glaze Coat.

GLOVES Unless you're leafing, applying tape, or using a pencil or small artist brush to make a design, wear gloves! Obviously, gloves keep your hands clean. But more important, gloves protect you from a wide variety of toxic elements that can enter the body through your fingernails and skin. Hardware stores sell all kinds of gloves and I use the green plastic disposable kind. Most pharmacies carry surgical gloves and although they tend to tear rather easily, they certainly improve control of your brushes. I even know people who use kitchen gloves—but whichever gloves you find or have, use them. *Any* glove is better than no glove at all.

GOLD SIZE is an adhesive used when leafing (because leaf will not stick by itself). It is available in a fast-drying water-based form which takes about 15 minutes to set up, a quick-drying synthetic form which takes about 2 hours to set up, and an oil-based form which takes about 12 hours. We talk about size "setting up" because you can only apply the leaf when the adhesive feels tacky (but not sticky or gooey to the touch). If you apply leaf to size before it has set up properly (before it "reaches tack") it may stick, but it will lose its luster. The leaf will absorb the size and (what we call) "drown." You can actually work with water-based size up to 36 hours after application. I use the water-based size (with the 15-minute set-up time) and suggest you do the same if you can find it. Gold size can be purchased wherever you find leaf. Start asking at your local artist's supply, paint, or hardware store.

JAPAN DRIER is a liquid that accelerates the drying time of linseed oil. Since artist oils contain a good deal of linseed oil, we use Japan drier instead of waiting what seems like forever for an artist oil glaze to dry. Use two or three drops (only!). You can buy Japan drier in a hardware store.

LEAF Leaf comes in six materials: real gold, composition gold (sometimes called Dutch metal), real silver, aluminum (which has a silver color but doesn't tarnish), copper, and variegated. (Variegated leaf is composition gold leaf that has been heated, and the amount of heat yields gold and blue, gold and red, and gold and green colors.) These different leafs can

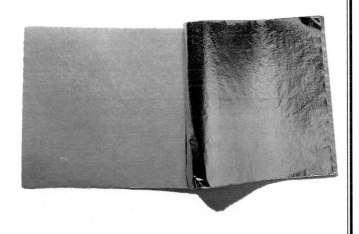

13

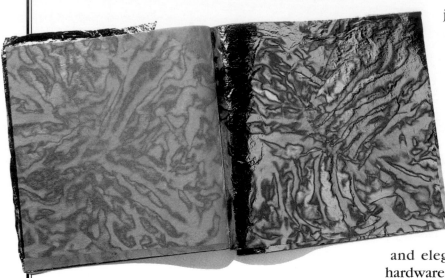

just tell the person you're buying it from how big your project is (then add another book for mistakes and the unexpected). Eventually, you'll be able to estimate quantities on your own.

LEMON OIL This is used as a fine furniture polish. (The oil nourishes the wood, which tends to dry out in heat and air conditioning.) We combine lemon oil with rotten stone (ground pumice) in a final sanding and polishing step. When buffed with a clean cloth, the mixture yields a beautiful and elegant sheen. You can buy lemon oil in a hardware store.

MINERAL SPIRITS A less toxic and (much) less expensive form of solvent than turpentine, it's easier to find in larger quantities. We use mineral spirits to thin oil-based paints or oil-based varnish, and for cleanup (brushes, spills, overlaps) of any oil-based materials. Mineral spirits can be found in hardware stores.

PAINT TYPES In this book, we use two types of paint: water base (latex and acrylic), and oil base (alkyd, Japan, and artist). Each type and grade of paint has its unique position in painted finishes, and one is chosen over another because it's the proper choice for the task.

Latex is easy on the environment, available in a great many colors and a wide range of cost, doesn't smell, and comes in matte, satin, and gloss finishes (plus new sheens like "enamel" and "pearlized" which keep hitting the market). I like the Benjamin Moore and Pratt & Lambert brands.

Acrylic is a fine artist's medium that comes in a *very* wide range of colors. Acrylics come in tubes and jars, are more expensive than latex, dry much faster, and also have no smell. With acrylics, I use the Windsor & Newton, Liquitex, and Hyplar (by Grumbacher) brands.

Alkyd is the least expensive oil paint, has a very wide range of colors to choose from, and can be bought in large quantities. Alkyd, like Japan and artist oils, has that old, familiar oil-paint smell. I like the Benjamin Moore and Pratt & Lambert brands.

Japan is the next step up in quality. This formulation originally came from Japan, is much finer but also more expensive than alkyd, and is sold in smaller quantities. Although the range of colors is

be purchased in artist's supply stores or leafing supply outlets like Sepp Leaf Products (their address and phone number is in the Source List at the end of the book).

We aren't using real gold in this book because the cost differential between it and composition (Dutch metal) gold is considerable.

For objects with flat surfaces, one layer of leaf is all you'll ever need. Objects with medium to heavy carving, however, will take two layers to get the coverage you want.

Leaf comes in "books" of 25 sheets, and in order to free the sheets, you must cut the selvage (binding) before starting a project. Each sheet comes sandwiched between two pieces of tissue paper. With composition gold (Dutch metal) and real silver, the tissue prevents the natural oils on your fingers from tarnishing the leaf. In the case of real gold (which doesn't tarnish), the tissue protects the leaf from disintegrating. With real gold or composition gold leaf, the tissue is a reddish color. It's called "rouge paper" because it actually contains a bit of rouge powder. Get in the habit of handling leaf with its tissue paper.

Whenever you leaf, excess gets rubbed off as part of the smoothing process. This excess is called "skewings" and you will use most of it before the project is finished. However, there's usually leftover, and should you join the thousands and thousands before you who have become addicted to leafing, make a skewings box. Simply, a skewings box (or jar) holds the excess leaf you will continually find invaluable for touch-ups. As you move from project to project, make a skewings box for each different type of leaf.

How much leaf will you need? At the beginning,

smaller, the colors are always consistent. I use the Chromatic and Ronan brands.

Artist is the best and most expensive grade of oil paint. It comes in tubes, uses the finest pigments, and takes the longest to dry. Since this is the *oil* fine artist medium, there are literally hundreds of colors from which to choose. The brands I prefer are Grumbacher and Windsor & Newton.

PAINT CONTAINERS When you get serious about painted finishes, you will no longer throw out *any* soup, dog, or cat food can; baby food jar; yogurt, sour cream, or cottage cheese carton; butter tub; or take-out food container. In fact, you will send word to your friends to save their's for you as well. (But please pick them up or else your friends will be stuck with empty containers and you'll be stuck with cranky friends.) When using either latex or acrylics, it's actually safe to use a piece of kitchenware as a container, as long as you wash out the paint while it's still wet.

RAGS Assemble a collection of old T-shirts, sheets, towels—almost anything will do that's 100 percent cotton. (Synthetic fabrics just don't absorb paint.)

ROTTEN STONE This is actually ground pumice, a dry pigment. It is brown-gray and can either be used to suggest a "dusty" color (when mixed with wax) or made into a paste with lemon oil (due to its "gritty" consistency) and used as a final sanding and smoothing step. Rotten stone can be found in hardware stores, and I like the Rainbow brand.

SAND FINISH Sand Finish is mixed with paint or

gold size to get a highly textured effect. The sand in sand finish is more coarse than typical beach sand, and it can be bought in hardware stores or paint stores geared toward professional painters.

SANDPAPER can be bought in any hardware store. The higher the number, the more sand per square inch, and the finer the paper. To find out more about sandpaper (and sanding), read the Preparation section on page 17.

SARAL PAPER is like carbon paper. It comes in many different colors and when you put it chalk side down and make an impression on the back (with a pencil, for example), the Saral paper transfers the chalk to the surface so you can follow a line or design. Saral paper can be found in artist's supply stores and occasionally in stationery stores.

SELVAGE is the binding that holds together a book of leaf.

SHELLAC is a gum resin that is dissolved in alcohol. It's a sealer that's also called "French varnish" or "French polish." This product was used universally until varnish came along, and since it's alcohol-soluble, all those rings you see on old furniture are the result of cocktail glasses thoughtlessly placed on shellacked surfaces. Any hardware store carries shellac.

TACK CLOTH can be purchased in hardware stores. It's actually cheesecloth dipped in shellac, and it's used to pick up dust from surfaces. A tack cloth should be kept sealed in a glass jar so it doesn't dry out, and it's no longer any good when you can see that it's dirty and it's lost its stickiness (its "tack.") Don't *ever* use a tack cloth on unprotected leaf because it will scratch the leaf off. (If the leaf is very dusty, use a soft, clean rag or brush.)

TAPE We use three types of tape in this book—masking, low-tack, and painter's.

Masking tape is the most commonly found and has the highest "tack" (meaning it's the most sticky). We use masking tape when we're not concerned about the possibility of a surface *lifting off* when we remove the tape.

Low-tack tape is less easy to find and less sticky. It's often blue in color and about three times as expensive as masking tape. If low-tack tape weren't so expensive, I'd probably recommend that you use it all the time.

Painter's tape is much less expensive and can be found in any hardware store. It's used by painters to protect straight lines on walls and other surfaces so only about $^1/_3$ of the back of it is sticky. Painter's tape is very low-tack and allows some seepage.

Note: In *all* instances with *all* tape, apply it *just before* you need it and remove it *immediately* after you've finished. This is because some of the glue on the tape can remain on your surface, especially in very hot or very cold weather. Then you will have to clean it off and—possibly—ruin what you've done.

Never leave tape on any longer than necessary—even if you have to retape at a later time.

UNIVERSAL TINTS These pigments made into liquid dyes are mixed into a medium of some kind (varnish, oil or water paint, glazecoat). They come in about twenty colors. We use universal tints to change colors, and when we have some white paint and our collection of tints, we can go anywhere and accomplish almost anything. I say accomplish *almost* anything because universal tints can't reach very dark intensities. They're fine, however, for light and medium colors. Universal tints are sold in paint stores.

VARNISH Varnish is used to protect finishes, and replaced shellac many years ago in serving that function. Varnish comes in oil- and water-based forms. Let's start with the oil-based. Oil-based var-

nish contains a resin, and it's this resin that dries, hardens, and protects. Oil varnish provides a stronger and smoother finish than water-based, and comes in high gloss, satin, and matte, and smells like, well, like oil varnish.

High-gloss is oil varnish in its purest form. You never need to stir it, and you must *never* shake it (this causes bubbles that are very hard to get rid of). High-gloss oil varnish provides a lacquerlike finish.

Satin oil varnish is less shiny than high-gloss and is made by adding a little wax. The wax, however, settles to the bottom of the can, so you must stir it well before using it (but still, never shake it).

Matte oil varnish has no shine and, therefore, contains more wax than satin. Not only must matte oil varnish be stirred before using, it must be *re*stirred if you let it sit for more than 30 minutes.

Because of the wax, satin and matte oil varnish do not sand very well when we "tuff-back" (see page 19.) Oil varnish yellows. Despite what it might say on the can, there is only *more yellowing* or *less yellowing*. If you're applying oil varnish to a dark surface, this doesn't matter very much. But if you're applying it to a light surface, either take the yellowing into account or use water-base varnish. I use the McCloskey (Heirloom) brand because I've found that it yellows the least.

Water-base varnish doesn't yellow, doesn't smell, and dries faster than oil. It also comes in gloss, satin, and matte finishes but it isn't as strong as its oil counterpart. (It scratches easier and many of the scratches won't sand off.) Also, it isn't as easy to apply on large surfaces. It must be mixed well before using, but again, don't shake.

It's important to consider that water-base varnishes are more ecologically friendly than oil varnishes—you just clean them up with water. (By contrast, oil-based varnish must be cleaned with mineral spirits.) I prefer Benjamin Moore latex urethane, or Verathane's Diamond brand. A paint store will be your source for varnish, either oil- or water-based.

PREPARATION

*t*HERE'S NO GETTING AROUND IT. PREPARATION IS THE DULLEST PART OF PAINTED FINISHES. BUT EVEN THOUGH THIS IS TRUE, WHATEVER TIME PUT IN IS *NEVER* WASTED. IF YOU DON'T PREPARE AN OBJECT PROPERLY AT THE BEGINNING, YOU WILL BE VERY DISAPPOINTED AT THE END. LET'S TAKE A WOODEN BOX FOR EXAMPLE, ANY WOODEN BOX. IT HAS TO BE CLEANED FIRST WITH ALCOHOL AND CLEAN RAGS TO REMOVE ACCUMULATED GREASE AND DIRT. IT HAS DEEP NICKS AND SCRATCHES, AND FILLER HAS TO BE APPLIED, ALLOWED TO DRY, THEN SANDED AS SMOOTH AS THE SURROUNDING AREAS. A TACK cloth removes dust—and only then is the piece ready for shellac and a base coat or two.

This work took about thirty minutes, maybe an hour or more, and yes, it was boring. But if it hadn't been done, the shellac, paint, and finish would *highlight* everything that was wrong with the box to begin with. The nicks and scratches would become **NICKS AND SCRATCHES**, the dust would be there (and visible) forever, and not only that, with enough grease and dirt on the box to begin with, you would now be looking at a very uneven finish.

You know yourself, so make a judgment about how much work you're willing to invest in any given piece. This is especially true if you're just starting out. Do not choose a piece that needs a great deal of preparation for one of your first projects. For example, the Venetian mirror frame (Recipe 18 on page 105) took an enormous amount of preparation. I had to sand off all the black, gooey glue that held the mirror in place, pull out tiny glass fragments all around the interior, fill large holes, sand the entire thing smooth, and shellac it. If you were just starting out and had chosen this piece, the preparation might have turned you *off* before the finish could turn you *on*.

Also, choose a piece you like, one that has charm or will be very useful once finished. You will work hard and invest creative energy in any piece you choose to do—so make sure it's worth the effort.

Getting Started

Newspaper is the perfect material to cover your work surface for all the obvious cost and accessibility reasons. Put down three or four layers before you begin (the layers will enable you to get a clean surface whenever you want).

This is a good time to reemphasize the use of gloves, for all the reasons I mentioned in the Materials section (page 13). Gloves not only keep your hands clean, they also protect you from all sorts of chemicals that are better off in the cans of the products we use than in your bloodstream. Use gloves, please.

Speaking of protection, don't forget to protect your floor and the surrounding environment (with newspapers and/or a plastic drop cloth). And also be smart about what to wear (an apron, and sneakers or shoes you don't care about).

Finally, choose a well-ventilated area for your work space. Although none of the products we use

in this book is actually dangerous, there's no reason to breathe their fumes if you don't have to. If you're very concerned about fumes, masks are available in paint and hardware stores.

The Project Itself

One of the first steps to take with *any* piece is to remove everything you can that you don't intend to decorate, like a mirror or picture, and the hardware (drawer pulls, hinges, if possible, and so on.) Put the mirror or picture in a safe place and put all the hardware in a sealed and labeled envelope. (I learned the importance of doing this the hard way. Can you imagine the feeling of misplacing a one-of-a-kind eighteenth-century drawer pull?) It's also at this stage when you can start thinking about replacing hardware that may no longer go with the piece you're about to create. And, if any part of the piece is loose, this is the moment to fix it. (If you've used glue, wait for it to dry thoroughly before moving on to any next steps.)

Tip: When working on any small object, you might want to use a lazy Susan. This way, you can turn *it* instead of constantly handling the object. Just protect its surface with layers of newspaper and you can get right to work.

Filling

As you look at your piece, you might see nicks, gouges, or scratches that are too deep to be sanded away, or, if you've removed hardware you don't intend to reinstall, there are likely to be large nail or screw holes. This is when you would use filler. All fillers can be applied with a knife, a spatula, or even your finger. After the filler has dried, it must be sanded smooth, that is, flush with the rest of the surface. (This is a very easy sanding job. Just use #280 sandpaper and apply gentle pressure.) Filler must be *sealed* before going on to any next step, therefore apply a coat of shellac with a small bristle brush and let dry for 20–30 minutes.

Tip: if you're working on an exposed corner, add a drop of Borden's water-soluble glue to the filler before applying it. The glue will make the mixture stronger and more able to stand up to a knock or two. **Warning:** Paint will not (repeat, not) fill in a surface you'd rather not bother filling and sanding. If its a hole/nick/scratch now, it will be a hole/nick/scratch later—with a brand-new color calling everyone's attention to it.

Sanding

After you've removed all the hardware you can, scrape and sand any peeling paint.

Before you begin to sand, get all your brushes, tack cloths, and paint cans out of the way. (You don't want dust on or in any of them.) Always sand in the direction of the grain of the wood, or *choose* a direction if the grain is covered with paint or decoration. Be sure to select the right grade of sandpaper for the job you're doing, and if you're just beginning, describe the piece and its condition to someone at your hardware/paint store and follow his or her advice. (After a while, you'll come to know what grade of paper is right for what kind of job.) To get you started, however, we basically use only four different grades of sandpaper in *Fantastic Painted Finishes*.

1. #100 is as coarse a grade as we ever use. (Remember, the number equals the number of grains of sand per inch. The more grains, the higher the number, and the finer the paper.) Use #100 when you have to remove very thick chipped paint.

2. #180 sandpaper is used to remove normal peeling paint. It's a finer paper than #100 and it not only sands but also begins the smoothing process.

3. #280 paper is used if the surface you're starting with is relatively smooth. It's also used to sand filler after it's dry.

4. #400 and #600 are wet/dry sandpapers (which yes, can be used either wet or dry). I do a sanding step a few times in the book that involves wet/dry sandpaper. Although I never name the process in the recipes, it's actually called "tuff-backing." We tuff-back in order to cut through the surface of paint or varnish to create a smooth, glasslike finish. (You will love the result.) We use #400, then #600 wet/dry paper in this process and do it only with oil-based products. You will know you're tuff-backing properly when you experience a "sucking" sensation as you apply the moistened sandpaper to a surface.

You will learn very quickly whether you have a "light" or "heavy" hand when using these papers. If you have a light hand, start with #400 and then move onto #600. If you have a heavy hand, never touch the #400—before you know it, you will go right through the finish down to bare wood.

When sanding, use your whole body and get into a rhythm. If you use your arm only, it will put pressure on your elbow and soon become unpleasant.

Do this often enough and you can actually develop a case of tendonitis. Even though it's natural to want to complete this process quickly, don't rush. You will get much better results with a slow and steady pace. And be very careful with electric sanders. You really have to know what you're doing with an electric sander or else you'll remove much too much surface.

Tip: If you're trying to sand into grooves, try wrapping a piece of #280 sandpaper over the round end of an artist brush. You can also wrap it around one of your fingers, or even fold it in half and use it this way. If you're sanding a large surface, buy what's called a "sanding block" in any hardware store. Although it's just a block of wood that you wrap sandpaper around, it's a great time-saver.

After you've finished sanding, dust your piece with a clean rag and get rid of the layer of newspaper you've been sanding on. Since the next step is shellacking, be sure to use a tack cloth on your object before proceeding.

A word here about tack cloths. An amazing amount of dust accumulates on surfaces in just a short period of time. Before any shellac, paint, or varnish step, use a tack cloth. This is especially true when you're working hard to achieve a smooth finish. If you don't use a tack cloth, you will not only be able to see dust under the final finish, you'll also be able to *feel* it.

Shellacking

Now it's time to shellac. Shellac is a sealer we apply after the cleaning, filling, and sanding steps.

Just as when sanding, always apply shellac in the direction of the grain. If you're working on an object that isn't wood, or on a wooden object where you can't see the grain, choose a direction and stick to it. Don't go back and forth over the shellac with your brush. (Shellac dries very quickly, and you'll make a gooey mess). If you missed some places, it's better to let it dry for 30 minutes and then apply a second coat. After the shellac is dry, you're ready to base-coat. However, if your first coat has created ridges, gently rub with 0000 steel wool then use a tack cloth.

Base Coating

Always make sure the paint you're applying is the right consistency. If the paint is too thin, you won't get enough coverage, and if the paint is too thick, you'll get brush marks ("grooves") in the finish.

Note: Whenever diluting paint, wait about 15

minutes for the ingredients to integrate fully. This will ensure you have a true consistency.

If you're applying more than a single coat of paint, always tightly cover the paint can while waiting for the coat to dry. If you're using the same color oil paint, you don't have to clean your brush between coats. Just wipe off the excess on a rag, shape the bristles to make sure they're flat, then wrap the brush in aluminum foil (tight enough to close out the air, but still keeping the shape of the brush). Place the brush in your refrigerator or freezer and take it out again when you're ready for the next coat. (Since it's so easy to clean wet latex paint off brushes, just wash them under running water between coats.

Always paint from the top of a piece to the bottom. This will enable you to catch any drips. Never dip more than one-third of the brush into the paint. If you put the brush *all* the way in, paint will get up and under the ferrule (the metal band that holds the bristles) and it's almost impossible to clean. (What usually happens then is that the paint that's hiding in there waits until you're painting a large white surface to make its reappearance. So unless you like the idea of white with stripes of another color, never put your brush all the way into paint.)

Preparation is a step with no flash and dazzle—but it's when the piece really becomes *yours*.

VARNISHING

VARNISHING IS BOTH THE FINAL PROTECTIVE STEP AND A VISUAL STEP. AS A PROTECTIVE STEP, UP TO 6 COATS DO JUST FINE. IF YOU'VE COMPLETED A SIDE TABLE, FOR EXAMPLE, FROM 3 TO 6 COATS WILL PROTECT ITS TOP FROM THE USUAL WEAR AND TEAR. THE LEGS WILL NEED NO MORE THAN 2 COATS (BUT UNDERSTAND THAT VARNISH WON'T HELP VERY MUCH IF YOU'RE IN THE HABIT OF SLAMMING YOUR VACUUM CLEANER AROUND).

AS A VISUAL STEP, YOU CAN VARNISH UP TO 20 COATS (FOR THE LOOK OF JAPANESE LACQUER). INTERESTINGLY, THOUGH, THIS MANY COATS PROVIDES LESS RATHER THAN MORE PROTECTION. THE VARNISH BECOMES FRAGILE— YOU CAN CHIP IT, OR EVEN CRACK IT STRAIGHT DOWN TO THE BASE coat if you knock it hard enough. don't overvarnish unless you're looking for a specific visual effect.

Oil-base varnish is stronger than water-base, therefore we use it when we want a good deal of protection. We also use it when we "tuff-back" (see page 19). You also might want to review the information on Varnish in the Materials section (page 16). Remember, unlike water-based, all oil-based varnish yellows. The higher quality the varnish, the less yellowing—but it's just a question of *how much* with each particular brand.

As I said earlier, the environmental movement has grown in size and political clout, and this has caused varnish manufacturers to respond. I've been seeing a wide variety of varnish formulations hitting the market, so what used to be a simple choice between oil- and water-based is simple no longer. My best advice if you can't find the brands I've recommended (McCloskey Heirloom for oil-based, and Benjamin Moore latex urethane or Verathane Diamond for water-based), is to find someone at your paint/hardware store who seems knowledgeable and ask for advice about price, quality, protection, and application. After you've tried a few oil- and water-based brands, you will find the ones that work best for you. Also, *always read and follow all the label instructions*.

Buy oil varnish in the smallest quantities you can because it goes bad when left unused. (How long this takes depends on how much varnish versus how much air is in the can, plus the climate where you live—but about six months is a round figure.) You'll know the varnish is bad if it's thickened and looks cloudy. *Do not* use varnish in this state. Dispose of it (properly) and buy some more.

Note: Every part of the country has different local ordinances and rules about disposal of materials like varnish, and every apartment building has rules of *its* own as well. Over the course of time, you will be throwing away many cans of various substances, plus brushes, rags, and more. Much of this collection will either be flammable, be unfriendly to the environment, have fumes that can make people

dizzy, or all of the above. So please be responsible about disposal. Find out what the procedures are where you live—and abide by them. And never *ever* pour old varnish, paint, shellac, or other such liquids down your sink or into your toilet. Your plumbing and the environment will thank you.

When you work with oil-based varnish, use a natural oxhair or rabbit's hair brush, apply the varnish in the most comfortable direction, and feel free to move the brush back and forth as you work.

With water-based varnish, use a synthetic varnish brush; also go in a chosen direction, but don't brush back and forth because water-based varnish dries very quickly. Just apply the varnish in a single direction as you work across your piece.

Most of the rest of what I have to say about varnishing (with oil or water-based) is similar to what I said about preparation and base coating. Here are three "always" and one "never":

- **Always use a tack cloth before every fresh coat of varnish (except on unprotected leaf).**
- **Always varnish in a well-ventilated work area.**
- **Always apply varnish from the top of a piece to the bottom so you can easily deal with drips.**
- **Never place your brush more than one-third of the way into varnish. This will make cleanup much easier.**

If you're using oil-base varnish, you can use the "brush wrapped in tin foil and put in the freezer" trick (see Preparation, page 20).

Finally, if you're varnishing a carved piece, you will have to use your brush to pounce (push) the varnish into all the nooks and crannies (and then go back with your brush to smooth out the bubbles created by the pouncing). If your piece has ridges, the varnish will have a tendency to sit in there—then slowly drip out. So wait a few minutes after you're finished and take a look. If you need to, take a brush (with no new varnish on it) and go over the ridges.

CLEANUP

*i*F YOU'VE PROTECTED YOUR WORK SURFACE AND FLOOR, IF YOU'VE
PROTECTED YOUR SURROUNDING ENVIRONMENT, AND IF YOU'VE
WORN GLOVES—ALL THAT SHOULD BE LEFT TO CLEAN UP WILL BE
BRUSHES (AND OCCASIONALLY YOURSELF). LET'S LOOK FIRST AT
BRUSHES, AND WHAT YOU MIGHT HAVE BEEN APPLYING WITH THEM.

Brushes Used to Apply:

SHELLAC If you've used a poly brush, throw it away. It costs more in materials to clean a poly brush than to buy a new one. If you've used a bristle brush, place it in a can filled with enough denatured alcohol. Then dry it off with a clean rag, reshape the bristles, and stick it into another can (bristle side up) to dry.

OIL PAINT Wipe off the surface paint on a piece of newspaper, then swirl the brush around in mineral spirits until all the paint is gone. Clean off the mineral spirits with a rag, place it in a second bath of clean mineral spirits, then wash the brush with soap and running water. Wash it well, until no more color comes out. (Here's a test to see if you listened to me about not sticking your brush too far into the paint. If you *didn't,* you'll be here for thirty minutes futilely trying to get all the color out.) Reshape the bristles and stick it into another can (bristle side up) to dry.

Note: *Never* use a wet brush (wet with water, that is) with oil paint. The old adage about oil and water not mixing is true.

LATEX AND ACRYLICS Always clean these brushes in running water while they're still wet with paint. When latex paint dries (and it will dry on your brushes rather quickly), it becomes alcohol-soluble, and if not too dry, can be cleaned with denatured alcohol. There are various products on the market that can help clean dried paint out of brushes, but it's an unnecessary hassle and expense. Just don't let it happen.

VARNISH With water-based varnish, clean your brushes as if you were using latex or acrylic paint; with oil-based varnish, clean them as if you were using oil paint.

Your Clothes and Yourself

If you happen to get oil paint or oil varnish on your skin (even though you've been using gloves), mineral spirits, a clean rag, then soap and water will clean it off. If it's latex or acrylic paint, or water-based varnish, use soap and water and a small scrub brush (and if the paint has dried, it will actually peel off). On your nails, use nail polish remover. Finally, shellac will clean off with denatured alcohol.

Be careful where you put down your brush when the phone rings. If you have a dog, I guarantee that at least once, the brush will go directly into the dog's mouth, and then the paint on the brush will be deposited all over your walls (doggy-height) when you return. Plus, the paint isn't any better in your pet's stomach than it is in yours.

In terms of clothes, you may luck out with latex or acrylic paints if you wash them immediately. (Yes, immediately. And while you're changing, you might ask yourself why you were wearing something good enough to care about in the first place!) Oil-based products are trickier, however, and you must take whatever article of clothing it is to the cleaners and tell them what the smear is made of. Then keep your fingers crossed.

All the Rest of It

After you've finished the day's work session, be sure to close up your shellac, paint, and varnish cans by hammering around the edges of the lid. Air is an enemy of whatever's in the can so get a good tight seal (and do this with a rag covering the lid before you start banging away. If not, you'll have splatters everywhere).

The more you work with painted finishes, the better you will get at them. There are no secrets. They're all about paint. You put paint on . . . you take paint off . . . and if you don't like the result, you can start all over again. So pick a recipe and get started. In a few hours—in your kitchen, basement, dining room, or garage—you can create *magic.*

2
SMALL OBJECTS

Obelisk

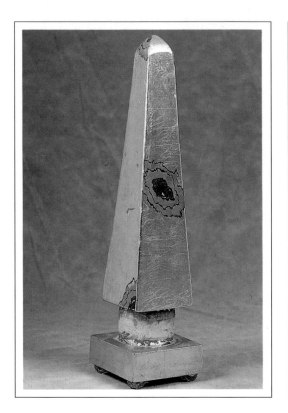 

*t*HIS OBELISK IS MADE OF WOOD AND I FOUND IT AT A GARAGE SALE (WITH A $3 PRICE TAG, NO LESS). NO ONE'S EVER GOING TO USE THIS OBJECT, THAT IS, WEAR IT, SERVE ANYTHING ON IT, OR HAVE IT PROP OPEN A DOOR. ITS SOLE FUNCTION IS TO STAND SOMEWHERE AND LOOK ABSOLUTELY FABULOUS. WITH THIS IN MIND, I AM CHOOSING A PURE-LY DECORATIVE FINISH THAT NEVER FAILS TO CATCH THE EYE.

RECIPE 1: OBELISK

Finish

Tortoiseshell on Gold Leaf

Time

Working time: a little over 3 hours
Total time (including drying): about 2½ days
and 9½ hours

At a Glance

1. Clean the obelisk (5 minutes)
2. Apply base coat (10 minutes)
3. Let dry (2 hours)
4. Apply second base coat (10 minutes)
5. Let dry (2 hours)
6. Apply gold size (10 minutes)
7. Let dry (15 minutes minimum)
8. Leaf (1 hour)
9. Tortoiseshell the darker shapes (1 hour)
10. Let dry (24 hours)
11. Tortoiseshell the lighter shapes (15 minutes)
12. Let dry (24 hours)
13. Varnish (10 minutes)
14. Let dry (4 hours)

Materials

General

gloves, clean cotton rags, water, containers, stirrers, scissors, tack cloth, 4 jar tops to raise obelisk off work surface

Preparation

alcohol
flat latex paint—red clay
2″ poly brush

Gold Sizing

quick-drying size (water-base if you can find it)
1″ and 2″ poly brushes

Leafing

10 sheets of composition leaf (Dutch metal)
2″ soft bristle brush
cotton (a handful)

Finishing: Tortoiseshell

artist oil—burnt umber
#6 round sable brush
#3 soft round badger brush (or soft makeup brush)
mineral spirits

Varnishing

water-base varnish—gloss
2″ oxhair brush

Comments and Tips

• Before you begin this finish, you might want to practice drawing all the tortoiseshell shapes and designs. Use a crayon, felt-tip marker, or—best of all—black paint and a brush. Take a look at the step-by-step photos and try your hand at the elongated *C,* the backward *C,* the funny-looking *9,* and the various dots and lines. If these shapes remind you of an inkblot test, then you're really in the spirit of doing tortoiseshell.

• As with all the finishes in this book, you *can* do tortoiseshell—but it might take a little practice before you can do it the way you want. Don't be hard on yourself if this is your first time. Trust me, you cannot fail—everyone will know your object is tortoiseshell. In fact, the real McCoy often looks like a painted finish.

STEP BY STEP

1 Clean the obelisk with alcohol and a clean rag. Use 4 jar tops to raise it off the work surface to reach the bottom edges. Apply a coat of flat latex bole (red clay color) with a 2″ poly brush and let dry for 2 hours.

2 When the first coat is dry, use a tack cloth to remove the accumulated dust and apply a second coat. After letting dry for 2 hours, you're ready for finishing.

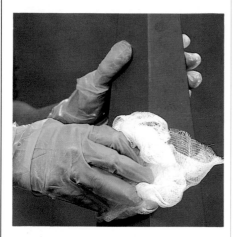

3 Apply an even coat of gold size with a 1″ poly brush. Gold size is an adhesive, and leaf won't stick to any surface without it. You always apply gold size (and you always leaf), from the bottom of a piece to the top. This is because if you started leafing at the top, all the pieces that fall off as part of the process would land in unleafed places and stick in the size. Then, when you leafed over them, the finish would be lumpy. (This lumpiness is also why you apply an *even* coat of size. If you didn't, you would see "ridges" of it under the leaf.)
Tips: Don't underload your brush—you want to coat the

ntire surface. But don't overload it either—this will cause drips you have to touch up.

• Quick-drying size is wonderful because it's ready to be leafed in no time—but it also has a tendency to form small bubbles. The more gentle you are when applying it, the fewer bubbles you will have. Both bubbles and drips can also be seen in the final finish, so smooth them out now. Look for them especially around the bottom edges.

• Make sure you get size into the joint where the top of the obelisk meets the base (use the tip of the poly brush for this).

When you get to the upper section of the obelisk, switch to the 2″ poly brush. It will save time.

4 After you've finished applying gold size, wait a minimum of 15 minutes for it to set up (or 2 hours if not using water-base). When the size has achieved the right "tack," your index finger will not glide easily over the surface, but neither will it stick.

5 Before you begin to leaf, change the newspaper on your work surface. The only size you want around is what's already on the obelisk. Remove your gloves.

6 Take a book of Dutch metal composition leaf and cut off the binding to free

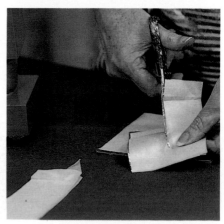

the individual sheets. We will use 10 sheets here. Cut 3 of them into thirds and set aside.

7 Start working from the bottom. Pick up a one-third sheet of leaf between its two pieces of rouge paper. Move close to the obelisk and let the front piece fall away. Press the leaf into the surface by rubbing your finger along the back of the rouge paper. Press along its

full length so the leaf folds around the edges.

Leaf all around the base and the circular area in the middle, then move upward. Use full sheets as you get to the column. Cover as much area as you can, but don't worry about missed places—you will come back at the end to touch up. And don't rush; although leafing takes patience, it's not difficult.

8 When you have leafed the entire obelisk, take your 2″ soft bristle brush and gently begin to smooth the areas where two leaves have overlapped. Brush in the direction of the overlap. (If you don't, you might tear the leaf.) This step smoothes the seams, joins them, and gently rubs off the excess leaf.

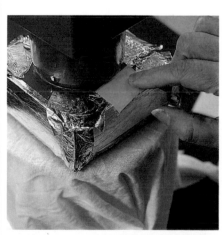

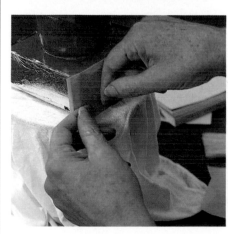

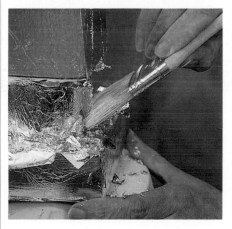

9 All the excess pieces that fall to the base as a result of this process are called "skewings." They can be picked up with your brush and placed wherever you need them. As long as there is gold size on the obelisk, you can use almost all the skewings for touch up.

Tip: Don't forget to leaf the underside of the obelisk, the area where the top joins the circular area in the middle. Small objects like this are enormously appealing. People tend to pick them up and handle them. So knowing this, always be sure that an entire piece is beautifully finished.

10 As a final leafing step, take a piece of cotton and rub it over the entire surface. Although you must be gentle until the obelisk is protected by varnish, this step adds a final smoothing.

Warning: Until Dutch metal leaf is protected by varnish, the oil from your hands will stain it. So, when handling the obelisk, do so with either a clean rag or a piece of rouge paper.

11 When the obelisk has been smoothed, clean off your work surface. If you intend to leaf often, place all the remaining skewings in a separate box.

12 With this particular tortoiseshell design, we will create the dark areas first and then add the lighter ones. We will use a burnt umber artist oil.

13 Squeeze 1″ of burnt umber into a container and use a #6 round sable brush to make the shapes you've practiced. Refer to your sketches and the step-by-step photos. As you go, use a #3 soft round badger brush to soften and smooth. The more times you make these shapes, the more confident you'll be, so if you'd rather practice some more before proceeding, fine.

14 Decorate the column and the base. For contrast, I've decided to leave the middle area plain gold.

15 Let the obelisk dry for 24 hours.

16 When the obelisk is dry, squeeze 2″ of burnt umber into a container and put a splash of mineral spirits into another container. Using your #6 round sable brush, dip first into the mineral spirits and then into the burnt umber. This is going to "wash out" the intensity of the color.

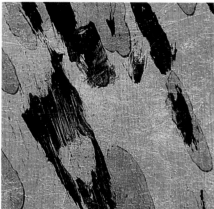

Swish the brush back and forth on your newspaper until the excess color is removed, go over the dark shapes already on the obelisk, and make new shapes in the middle of two existing ones. (Join them to fill in some of the empty spaces.) Use the #3 soft badger brush to shape and soften.

Connect the shapes in the most boring areas and leave the interesting areas alone. If you see any drips, whisk them away with the badger brush.

Real tortoiseshell is layered in design, and this is what we're simulating by putting the lighter shapes on top of the darker ones.

Apply the lighter shapes to the column and to the base. When you're finished, let dry for 24 hours.

Note: Being "finished" is an artistic judgement. Don't hesitate to make it.

Finally, apply a coat of gloss water-base varnish with a 2″ oxhair brush and let dry for 24 hours.

Now the fun begins. Walk your obelisk from room to room. A certain spot will "speak out" and you'll know exactly where to place this beautiful piece.

TWO METAL BRACELETS

PPLYING FINISHES TO JEWELRY IS SO FAST AND EASY THAT AFTER YOU TRANSFORM THIS PLAIN BRACELET INTO A COUNTRY LAPIS MASTERPIECE YOU CAN *GILD* IT FOR A DRESSY AFFAIR TOMORROW. WHEN YOU REALLY START THINKING ABOUT FINISHES THIS WAY, ALL YOU NEED TO CREATE A SHOWSTOPPER IS A PIECE OF VERY INEXPENSIVE DIME-STORE JEWELRY. WITH BRACELETS, WOOD USUALLY WORKS BEST, BUT YOU CAN ALSO WORK WITH PLASTIC OR WITH METAL (AS WE'RE DOING HERE).

RECIPE 2: TWO METAL BRACELETS

Finish

Country Lapis

Time

Working time: about 40 minutes
Total time (including drying): about 9 hours

At a Glance

1. Clean bracelet (5 minutes)
2. Apply bonding liquid (5 minutes)
3. Let dry (30 minutes)
4. Apply base coat (5 minutes)
5. Let dry (2 hours)
6. Lapis (20 minutes)
7. Let dry (2 hours)
8. Varnish (5 minutes)
9. Let dry (4 hours)

Materials

General

gloves, clean cotton rags, water, containers, stirrers, tack cloth

Preparation

alcohol
bonding liquid
flat latex paint—light beige
1″ poly brush
1″ bristle brush

Finishing

acrylic paint—raw sienna
acrylic paint—Prussian blue
acrylic paint—ultramarine blue
acrylic paint—red oxide
flat latex paint—light beige
water-base varnish—gloss
#4 round acrylic artist brush
4 containers
plastic teaspoons
cotton (a handful)

Varnishing

water-base varnish—gloss
1″ poly brush

Comments

• I am finishing two bracelets here, but I've written the recipe for one. If you have two as well, just repeat the steps.

STEP BY STEP

1 Clean the bracelet with alcohol and a clean rag, then use another rag to apply a coat of bonding liquid. After that has dried for 30 minutes, use a 1″ poly brush to apply a coat of light beige flat latex. Let the paint dry for 2 hours.

Note: We're using bonding liquid to make sure the metal accepts the paint. You do the same thing if you are working with plastic. However, if you're working with wood, apply a coat of clear shellac with a 1" bristle brush instead. Let it dry for 30 minutes as well.

2 Use a tack cloth to remove all the dust and you're ready for finishing.

3 In 3 separate areas of your first container, put 1″ of raw sienna, 1 teaspoon of water-base varnish, and ½ teaspoon of water (don't worry, they won't all run together).

4 Take a piece of cotton and dip it into the water, into the paint, and into the varnish. Then dab color on about 70% of the bracelet.

5 Repeat this process with the Prussian blue. In 3 separate areas of your second container, put 1″ of Prussian blue, 1 teaspoon of water-base varnish, and ½ teaspoon of water. Dip another piece of cotton into the water, into the paint, and into the varnish. This time, cover about 30% of the surface, dabbing color where there's no sienna and *barely* into areas where there is.

6 Repeat with the ultramarine blue. In your third container, put 1″ of ultramarine blue, 1 teaspoon of water-base varnish, and ½ teaspoon of water. Dip more cotton into water, into paint, and into varnish. Cover about 20% of the surface, where there is no sienna or Prussian blue, and barely into areas where there *is*.

Note: I say "barely" because the blue and the sienna make green when mixed. A little green is okay, but this bracelet should be blue.

7 As you apply the 3 colors, vary the times you use paint alone with times you use paint mixed with varnish and water. Paint alone has a more intense color, and we want color variations. When you're finished, about 10% of the base coat should still be showing.

8 Now, take your #4 round acrylic artist brush, dip it directly into the tube of red oxide, and make a random and occasional red "dot." (I do mean occasional—be stingy.) Real lapis contains deposits of iron, and these red dots simulate how they look.

9 So, how do you like it? If the end-result is too blue, or "too anything," use a piece of cotton and any of your colors (including the light beige base coat) to touch up until the effect pleases you. Let the completed bracelet dry for 2 hours.

10 Use a tack cloth to remove the accumulated dust, then apply a coat of gloss water-base varnish with a 1″ poly brush and let dry for 4 hours. Finally, get dressed, go out, accept all compliments gracefully.

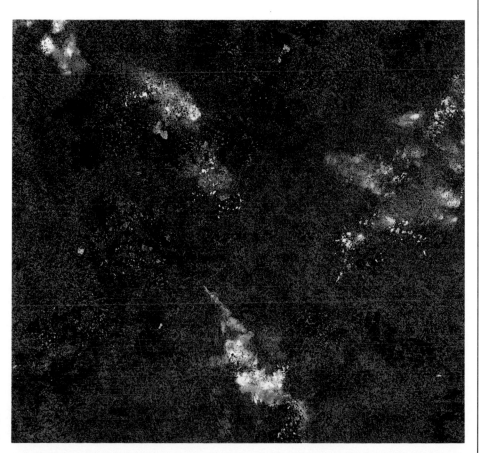

This is an example of a Lapis finish.

T R A Y

tHERE'S NO POLITE WAY TO SAY IT: THIS TRAY WAS BORING. IT WAS A UTILITARIAN OBJECT WITH NO LINE, NO DETAIL, AND NO DISTINGUISHING FEATURES WHATSOEVER. SO THE CHALLENGE HERE WAS TWO-FOLD: CHOOSE A FINISH THAT CAN STAND UP TO USE, AND DO SOMETHING (ANYTHING) TO MAKE THE TRAY INTERESTING.

RECIPE 3: TRAY

Finish
Porphyry with Tiger Stenciling

Time
Working time: about 1¾ hours
Total time (including drying): a little over
7 days

At a Glance
1. Clean the tray (5 minutes)
2. Apply base coat (10 minutes)
3. Let dry (2 hours)
4. Apply second base coat (10 minutes)
5. Let dry (2 hours)
6. Porphyry (20 minutes)
7. Let dry (24 hours)
8. Apply varnish (10 minutes)
9. Let dry (24 hours)
10. First stenciling step (10 minutes)
11. Let dry (24 hours)
12. Second stenciling step (5 minutes)
13. Let dry (30 minutes)
14. Last stenciling step (5 minutes)
15. Let dry (24 hours)
16. Varnish (10 minutes)
17. Let dry (24 hours)
18. Apply second varnish coat (10 minutes)
19. Let dry (24 hours)
20. Apply third varnish coat (10 minutes)
21. Let dry (24 hours)
22. Buff with clean rag (5 minutes)

Materials
General
gloves, clean cotton rags, water, containers, stirrers, scissors, 4 jar tops to raise tray off work surface
Preparation
alcohol
flat latex paint—dark beige (almost tan)
2″ poly brush

Finishing: Porphyry
Japan colors:
- C.P. green—light
- C.P. green—medium
- raw umber
- Prussian blue
- American vermillion
commercial alkyd paints (8 oz. cans)—white and black
5 spatter brushes or toothbrushes
5 additional jar tops
plastic teaspoons
mineral spirits
oil-base varnish—high gloss
2″ oxhair brush

Stenciling
3-step tiger stencil
painter's tape
oil-base paint—black
oil-base paint—yellow ocher
spatter brush or toothbrush
2 plastic teaspoons

Varnishing
oil base varnish—high gloss
2″ oxhair brush

Comments and Tips
• Porphyry is a very fine-grained granite found all over the world, and its color varies from place to place. The way we simulate porphyry in painted finishes is by spattering on layers of different color.

• Spatter finishes tend to get *everywhere;* so if you don't have a large work area, you might want to tape up some newspaper to protect any surrounding walls in "spatter distance."

• I'm using a precut tiger stencil here, but feel free to use whatever stencil you like. Stencils can be bought individually or in books at paint stores, artist's supply stores, and even some bookstores. I'm using a 2-step stencil—but so the tiger doesn't disappear into the background, I am also going tocreate an outline stencil as well. The difference in the steps is that each provides more detail and requires an additional layer of color.

STEP BY STEP

1 Clean the tray with alcohol and a clean rag, then use 4 jar tops to raise it off the work surface.

2 Use a 2″ poly brush and apply 2 coats of dark beige flat latex. Let each coat dry for 2 hours and you're ready for finishing.

3 In 4 jar tops, make 4 different glazes:

• ½ teaspoon of C.P. green—light, ⅛ teaspoon of raw umber (just the very tip of a spoon will do), 1½ teaspoons of white, and a drop of mineral spirits. Mix well.
• 2 teaspoons of straight black, and a drop of mineral spirits.
• ¼ teaspoon of Prussian blue, ¼ teaspoon of raw umber, 4 teaspoons of white, and a drop of mineral spirits. Mix well.
• ½ teaspoon of C.P. green—medium, the tip of a teaspoon of American vermillion, 2 teaspoons of white, and a drop of mineral spirits. Mix well.

4 To make life easy, place the paints and their individual spatter brushes from right to left in the order below (this will help avoid mixing up brushes and colors when you start working). Also, these are the coverages you want:
• Far right, C.P. green—light, 80% coverage
• Second from right, black, 50% coverage

• Third from right, Prussian blue, 70% coverage
• Far left, C.P. green—medium, 30% coverage

Note: Every time I say things like "80% coverage with this and 50% coverage with that" it makes me think of chemistry class. Well, porphyry isn't science—it's *art.* So please don't think you have to be tied exactly to proportions and percents. They're guidelines. Get started, take a look, and if you want something darker or lighter (or different in any way), simply adjust your paints accordingly.

5 Cover your containers so the color you're spattering doesn't mix with the others.

6 Ready to dive in? Put the tip of your first brush into the C. P. green—light, pat off excess paint on your newspaper, and spatter color onto the tray by pulling the bristles of the brush toward you. As you proceed, you will find that paint begins to accumulate on your "spattering finger"; wipe it off from time to time on your apron or work surface.

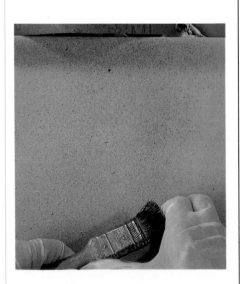

There is no need to wait between colors—just apply one on top of the other. Repeat this process with all 4 brushes and all 4 colors in the percentage of coverage I suggested.

Tip: If you get a large *blob* of paint instead of a spatter, place the edge of a tissue into the blob. The tissue will suck up the paint like a moist sponge. After a minute or two, spatter the area again.

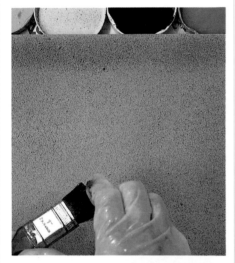

7 If you're almost finished and think you'd like another color variation, mix ½ teaspoon of black with ½ teaspoon of C. P. green—light. Spatter this at random.

8 Let dry for 24 hours.

9 Now apply a coat of high gloss oil-base varnish with a 2″ oxhair brush. Let dry for 24 hours.

10 The tiger stencil we're going to apply to this tray will simply disappear into the porphyry unless we give it its own background. In order to do this, we have to make another stencil—this one of the tiger's outline (or the outline of whatever you're using). So take a piece of paper, trace the shape of your object with a pencil, and carefully cut it out.

11 When you have made this new outline stencil, decide where you want to place your design. (As you can see from the photos, I'm going to stencil the tiger in two places.) When you've decided, tape the outline stencil down with painter's tape so it doesn't slip, and so that the rest of the tray is protected from stray spatters of color.

12 Pour 2 teaspoons of oil-base black into a container and 2 teaspoons of oil-base yellow ocher into another. With your 1″ spatter brush, spatter color into the cutout area of your new stencil. Spatter 90% yellow ocher and 10% black, one on top of the other. After you're finished, remove the stencil and let dry for 24 hours.

13 Carefully tape down step 1 of the tiger stencil you bought. Make sure you line up the new stencil on top of the outline. We're going to spatter two colors again, but this time it will be 90% of the black and 10% of one of the Prussian blue, raw umber, and white glaze from step 3. After you spatter on these two colors, carefully remove step 1 stencil, and let the paint dry for 30 minutes.

14 Just as carefully line up and tape down the step 2. This stencil will provide highlights on the tiger's face and paws, so spatter with white and then a little black. Remove the stencil. Wait 24 hours for the paint to dry.

15 Since we created porphyry by spattering layer upon layer of color, the tray will now be rough to the touch. How smooth you want it to be will dictate how many coats of varnish you're going to apply. Use high gloss oil-base varnish and a 2″ oxhair brush. Each coat will take 24 hours to dry, and you should apply a minimum of 3 coats.

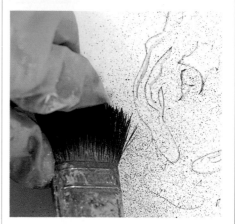

16 If you want the tray to be *really* smooth, do the following. After the third coat is dry, give the tray a once over with a moistened piece of #600 wet/dry sandpaper. After you've sanded it, apply 3 more coats of varnish (letting each dry for 24 hours). Sand again with #600 wet/dry, then apply one final coat with 50% varnish and 50% mineral spirits, letting it dry for 24 hours. If you've had your fill of varnishing, a final buffing with a clean cotton rag will do just fine.

17 Now, the pressure begins. Since the tray looks so fabulous, the food you serve *on* it has to measure up.

STATUE OF BUDDHA

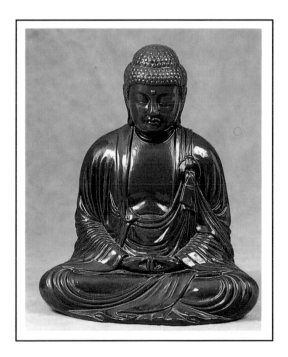 

*f*OR MOST PEOPLE, THIS STATUE IS DECORATIVE; FOR SOME, IT'S RELI-GIOUS—AND BOTH THESE ASPECTS MUST BE RESPECTED IF THE PIECE IS TO SUCCEED. I THOUGHT ABOUT THIS STATUE A GOOD DEAL BEFORE CHOOS-ING SILVER LEAF (BECAUSE OF ITS CLASSICAL AND UNIVERSAL ELEGANCE), PLUS ANTIQUING (TO MAKE IT SEEM AS IF THE BUDDHA WERE VERY OLD).

RECIPE 4: STATUE OF BUDDHA

Finish

Antiquing on Silver Leaf

Time

Working time: just over $1\frac{1}{2}$ hours
Total time (including drying): about 3 hours

At a Glance

1. Clean the statue (10 minutes)
2. Shellac (10 minutes)
3. Let dry (30 minutes)
4. Apply gold size (15 minutes)
5. Let dry (15 minutes minimum)
6. Leaf (30 minutes)
7. Shellac (10 minutes)
8. Let dry (30 minutes)
9. First antiquing step (20 minutes)
10. Let set up (20 minutes)
11. Second antiquing step (10 minutes)
12. Let dry (1 hour)
13. Buff (2 minutes)

Materials

General

gloves, clean cotton rags, water, containers, stirrers, scissors, tack cloth, 4 jar tops to raise the statue off work surface

Preparation

alcohol
clear, white shellac
1″ stiff bristle brush

Gold Sizing

quick-drying size (water-base if you can find it)
1″ stiff bristle brush
2″ soft bristle brush

Leafing

15 sheets of aluminum leaf
2″ soft bristle brush
1″ stiff bristle brush
cotton (a handful)

Shellacking

clear, white shellac
1″ bristle brush

Antiquing

butcher's wax
rotten stone
small palette knife
1″ stiff bristle brush
dry pigment—Venetian red
plastic teaspoons
newspaper (a few sheets)
mineral spirits

Comments

• We are using butcher's wax here, and you have to be very careful with it. You think oil and water don't mix? Well, butcher's wax and paint *really* don't. Paint will not stick wherever wax has been, so be sure to throw away any rags and newspaper you use with wax, plus the newspapers from your work surface, and your gloves. Also, be sure to clean your brushes with mineral spirits and then with soap and water.

STEP BY STEP

1 Clean the statue with alcohol and a clean rag, then use 4 jar tops to prop it off the work surface to get at the bottom edges.

2 The surface of the statue is in good shape, so we're going to apply shellac with a 1″ stiff bristle brush just to make sure it will accept a coat of gold size. Apply clear shellac and let dry for 30 minutes. After you use a tack cloth to remove the dust, you're ready for finishing.

3 Pour gold size into a container and to apply as even a coat as possible use a 1″ stiff bristle brush. Leaf won't stick to any surface without gold size. Always apply gold size and leaf from the bottom of a piece to the top. If you started leafing at the top, all the pieces that fall off as part of the process would land in unleafed places and stick in the size. When you leafed over them, the finish would be lumpy.

In carved areas (like the folds of the robe) it's almost impossible to apply an even coat, so apply size in the same direction as the folds. This way, if ridges *do* form,

they will be far less noticeable under the final finish. Take special care to get size into all the indentations on top of the head.

Quick-drying size is wonderful because it's ready to be leafed in no time, but it also has a tendency to form small bubbles. The more gentle you are when applying it, the fewer bubbles you will have. Both bubbles and drips can be seen in the final finish, so smooth them out now. Look for them especially around the bottom edges.

4 When you have finished applying gold size, wait a minimum of 15 minutes for it to set up (2 hours if not water-base). When the size has achieved the right "tack," your finger will not glide easily over the surface, but neither will it stick.

Before you begin to leaf, change the newspaper on your work surface and remove your gloves.

5 Take a book of aluminum leaf and cut the binding (the selvage) to free the individual sheets. We will be using about 15 sheets on the Buddha.

6 Pick up a sheet of leaf between its two pieces of tissue paper. Move close to

the back of the statue and let the front piece fall away. Press the leaf into the statue by rubbing your finger along the back of the tissue paper.

Work around the bottom, covering as much area as you can, then work upward. Don't worry about missed places—you will come back at the end to touch up. Do not rush. Leafing takes patience, but it's not difficult.

7 When you have leafed the entire statue, take your 2″ soft bristle brush and gently begin to smooth the areas where two leaves have overlapped. Move the brush in the direction of the overlap. (If you don't, you might tear the leaf and expose the surface underneath.) This brushing smoothes the seams, joins them, and rubs off the excess leaf (called "skewings").

8 When you have smoothed as much as possible, take a 1″ stiff bristle brush, pick up the skewings, and pounce them into all the carved areas. At least 2 layers of leaf will be needed in the folds of the robe, the details of the body and face, and the top of the head.

9 When you have smoothed and pounced as much as possible with both brushes, do a final smoothing with a piece of cotton rubbed over the entire surface.

10 Clean off your work surface, and if you intend to leaf often, place all the remaining skewings in your skewings box.

11 Now, apply a coat of clear shellac with a 1″ stiff bristle brush and let dry for 30 minutes.

12 After the shellac is dry, make a paste with 2 teaspoons of butcher's wax and 1 teaspoon of rotten stone. Mix it with a palette knife.

Then make another mixture—this one with 1 teaspoon of wax and 1 teaspoon of Venetian red pigment.

13 Start by dipping a 1″ stiff bristle brush into the rotten stone mixture. Tap off the excess on your newspaper, then pounce the mixture all over. It won't take long to notice that this gray color makes the statue look "cold," so begin to use some red (with the same brush). Although the overall effect should be gray, make the statue more red than gray in a few areas.

14 Wait 20 minutes so the wax gets a chance to set up a bit, then "scrunch" a piece of newspaper into a loose ball and take a strong swipe at a section of the statue. This will cause two things to happen: Wax will come off on the paper, and wax will really get pushed into the statue's folds and indentations. Keep doing this. Change the paper frequently, and after you get a feel for the process, decide how much wax you want to remove. More wax will look "crusty" and older, less will look "finer" and more used. Do not worry if some of the leaf is removed, it will add to the aged patina.

15 Let the wax dry for 1 hour, then do a final buffing with a soft cotton rag.

INKWELL

*t*HIS IS AN ORNATE PERIOD PIECE WITH SUCH LOVELY LINES THAT IT WILL BE ADMIRED WHEREVER ITS FINAL HOME HAPPENS TO BE. AFTER EVALUATING A FEW CHOICES OF FINISH, I DECIDED TO HIGHLIGHT THE INKWELL'S BEAUTY BY CONTRASTING GEM LAPIS WITH GOLD LEAF.

RECIPE 5: INKWELL

Finish

Gem Lapis and Gold Leaf

Time

Working time: about 3 hours

Total time (including drying): about 18 hours

At a Glance

1. Clean the inkwell (5 minutes)
2. Sand the surface (5 minutes)
3. Shellac (10 minutes)
4. Let dry (30 minutes)
5. Apply base coat (10 minutes)
6. Let dry (2 hours)
7. First lapis step (30 minutes)
8. Let dry (30 minutes)
9. Second lapis step (30 minutes)
10. Let dry (4 hours)
11. Varnish (10 minutes)
12. Let dry (4 hours)
13. Paint areas to be gilded (30 minutes)
14. Let dry (30 minutes)
15. Gold size (10 minutes)
16. Let dry (15 minutes minimum)
17. Leaf (15 minutes)
18. Varnish (10 minutes)
19. Let dry (4 hours)

Materials

General

gloves, clean cotton rags, water, containers, stirrers, scissors, tack cloth, 4 jar tops to raise inkwell off work surface

Preparation

alcohol

#240 sandpaper

clear, white shellac

two 1″ poly brushes

flat latex paint—pale blue

Finishing

acrylic paint—ultramarine blue

acrylic paint—Prussian blue

acrylic paint— white

acrylic paint—red oxide

2 small pieces of sea sponge

#4 artist bristle brush

#9 round acrylic brush

1″ poly brush

cotton (a handful)

bronze powder—gold

cheesecloth or sheer stocking

water-base varnish—gloss

4 additional jar tops

Gold Sizing

quick-drying size (water-base if you can find it)

1″ poly brush

Gilding

10 sheets of composition leaf (Dutch metal)

1″ soft bristle brush

Varnishing

water-base varnish—gloss

1″ poly brush

Comments and Tips

• You are creating a lapis finish here, and your eye knows what lapis looks like. Therefore, don't follow my instructions blindly. Trust your eye and follow what it tells you.

• Except on the unprotected leaf in this project, it is advisable to use a tack cloth to remove accumulated dust before any shellac, paint, or varnish step. (A tack cloth will scratch or even lift off unprotected leaf.)

STEP BY STEP

1 Clean the inkwell with alcohol and a clean rag, then sand it just enough to smooth and clean the surface.

2 Use 4 jar tops to raise it off the work surface so you can get at the bottom edges, then apply a coat of clear shellac with a 1″ poly brush. Let dry for 30 minutes.

3 Apply pale blue flat latex to the entire inkwell with a ″1 poly. Let the paint dry for 2 hours.

4 Squeeze out 1″ of ultramarine blue into a jar top, and 1″ of Prussian blue into another. Thin the Prussian blue with about 3 drops of water.

5 Dampen a sea sponge and dip it lightly into the ultramarine blue. You want just the peaks, points, and tips of the sponge in the paint. Tap the sponge onto the surface of the inkwell. Tap it lightly, so the points and peaks don't flatten out. You want about 70% coverage.

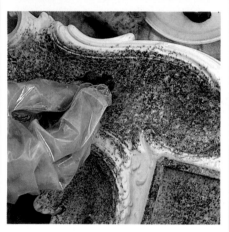

6 Dampen a second sponge, and do the same steps with the Prussian blue. This time, however, cover only about 30% of the surface.

7 Squeeze out another ½″ of Prussian blue into a separate container. We want areas of darker blue in the inkwell, so, using the same sponge, apply the straight Prussian blue—but to no more than 20% of the surface.

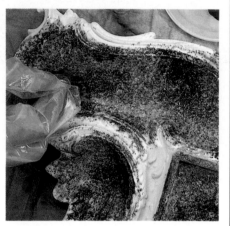

8 After you complete this sponging step, the surface will show the pale blue base coat, plus the ultramarine and Prussian blues we just applied.

Let the inkwell dry for 30 minutes.

9 Squeeze about ¼″ of white acrylic into a container. Take your #4 artist bristle brush and dip it into water, then into paint. (You want the paint to be "runny.")

In the *lightest* areas of blue, paint a maximum of 3 little white "clouds," then shape and flatten them by patting with a piece of cotton. Also try this: gently blow into one of the clouds to disperse the color. (Then use cotton to shape and flatten.) The drifts of white we're creating are called "matrixes." In real lapis, a matrix is an imperfection in the stone.

Since we're working with acrylics, if you don't like a matrix you've done (or if you've done too many) immediately use water and a clean rag to remove them. If the matrix has already dried, simply sponge some blue over it. Clean the brush under running water.

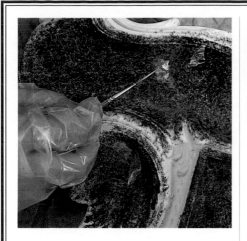

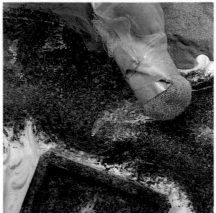

10 Now, with the same #4 artist bristle brush, place a dab of gloss water-base varnish where it's *darkest* blue. Sprinkle on a light dusting of gold bronze powder. (Pour bronze powder into the end of rolled-up cheesecloth or sheer stocking and tap it gently over the varnish.) This simulates the pyrite, or "fool's gold," that appears in lapis.)

Pick up the inkwell and move it back and forth to disperse the powder. Or pick it up and blow into it. We want to achieve the same visual effect as the white matrixes.

Reminder: The white matrixes go into the *lightest* areas of blue and the gold bronze powder into the *darkest*.

11 Let dry for 4 hours.

12 Apply a coat of gloss water-base varnish with a 1″ poly brush, and let the varnish dry for 4 hours.

13 Use a #9 round acrylic brush and paint the areas to be leafed with acrylic red oxide paint. We're using this red paint because it will enhance the brilliance of the leaf that's going over it. We just varnished the inkwell, so if you make any slips with the paint, use a piece of cotton and some water to clean them off. Let the paint dry for 30 minutes.

14 Apply an even coat of gold size with a #7 round acrylic brush. Get full coverage. Leaf will not stick to itself, so wherever there isn't size (or isn't enough), the leaf will fall off. Try to keep the size to nonlapis areas but don't use masking tape. It's too hard to apply on a piece this small, and even with low-tack tape, you run the risk of pulling off the finish.

15 Let the size set up for a minimum of 15 minutes (or 2 hours if not water-base). When the size has achieved the right "tack," your index finger will not glide easily over the surface, but neither will it stick. Change the newspaper on your work surface before you begin to leaf; the only size you want around is what's already on the inkwell. Also, remove your gloves—you need full dexterity for leafing.

16 As the size is drying, take a book of Dutch metal composition leaf and cut off the selvage to free the individual sheets. We will need about 10 sheets to complete the inkwell.

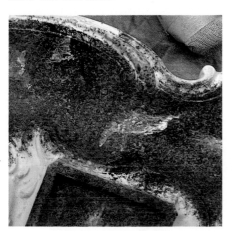

17 After the gold size is ready, pick up a sheet of leaf between its two pieces of rouge paper. Let the top piece fall away and slide it about ½" *under* the inkwell. Then, fold it up and over the top. There will be too much leaf when you do this, so use the rouge paper to double the leaf over on top of itself. This will create the 2 layers of leaf needed to cover these areas properly.

Note: The oils from your fingers will stain this leaf, so always handle it with rouge paper

Go all around the base of the inkwell in the same manner, overlapping the leaves slightly.

After the bottom is fully covered, take 2 sheets of leaf and cut them into quarters. Use these quarter sheets to leaf the carved *inside* portions of the inkwell. Cover all the surfaces, and use the rouge paper to press leaf into the indentations.

18 Now take your 2" soft bristle brush and "pounce" the leaf. Pick up all the excess (the skewings) and pounce them in where needed. You can also add more size and more leaf to any missed areas.

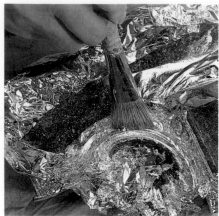

19 After most of the skewings are removed and pounced in, begin to smooth the piece by rubbing the brush into the leaf. Follow the direction of the carving all around so the leaf works its way into every surface.

20 Clean off your work surface and save your skewings for future leafing.

21 Apply gloss water-base varnish over the entire surface with a 1" poly brush. Let dry for 4 hours.

CANDLESTICKS

i WANTED TO GIVE A PAIR OF CANDLESTICKS AS A PRESENT TO NEWLY WED FRIENDS AND LOOKED A LONG TIME TO FIND A PAIR THAT WAS INTERESTING. WHEN I SPOTTED THESE IN A FLEA MAR- KET (FOR $5!), I WAS GLAD I'D KEPT LOOKING. THEY'RE CERAMIC, WERE MADE IN ITALY, AND LOOKED QUITE SPECTACULAR WHEN WE FINISHED THEM.

RECIPE 6: CANDLESTICKS

Finish

Black and Gold Marble (Portoro)

Time

Working time: almost 3 hours
Total time (including drying): 20 hours

At a Glance

1. Clean the candlesticks (5 minutes)
2. Shellac (10 minutes)
3. Let dry (30 minutes)
4. Apply base coat (10 minutes)
5. Let dry (4 hours)
6. Apply second base coat (10 minutes)
7. Let dry (4 hours)
8. Apply first half of finish (20 minutes)
9. Let dry (4 hours)
10. Apply second half of finish (1½ hours)
11. Let dry (30 minutes)
12. Varnish (10 minutes)
13. Let dry (4 hours)
14. Apply second varnish coat (10 minutes)
15. Let dry (4 hours)

Materials

General

gloves, clean cotton rags, water, containers, stirrers, tack cloth, 6 jar tops to raise candlesticks off work surface

Preparation

alcohol
clear, white shellac
1″ bristle brush

flat latex paint—black
1″ acrylic brush

Finishing

acrylic paint—white
acrylic paint—black
acrylic paint—raw umber
acrylic paint—yellow oxide
acrylic paint—raw sienna
#9 round acrylic brush
#4 acrylic brush
1″ soft sable brush
water-base varnish—gloss

Varnishing

water-base varnish—gloss
1″ acrylic brush

Comments and Tips

• As you can see, I am decorating these candlesticks while they lay on their sides (as opposed to working with them in an upright position). Do what's most comfortable for you.

• Portoro marble is different from other marbles in that its drifts run in parallel grooves (like train tracks). Even though the drifts sort of meander their way down (they are by no means ruler straight), they are still parallel. Furthermore, the "clouds" in the drifts run in a single direction, yellow veins follow the clouds, and an occasional white vein runs in a counter direction. All this would be much easier to see on a flat piece of portoro, but then we wouldn't have these wonderful curvy candlesticks.

• Before any shellac, paint, or varnish step, it is advisable to use a tack cloth to remove accumulated dust.

STEP BY STEP

1 Clean the candlesticks with alcohol and a clean rag. Apply clear shellac with a 1″ bristle brush. Let the shellac dry for 30 minutes, then apply 2 coats of flat black latex paint with a 1″ acrylic brush. Let each coat dry for 4 hours.

2 In a container, mix 1 teaspoon of acrylic white, the tip of a spoon of acrylic black, ½ teaspoon of acrylic raw umber, and 1 teaspoon of gloss water-base varnish. You want a mixture with the consistency of light cream, so thin with water (a little at a time) until you have it.

3 The first step is to make "cloud" shapes using a #9 round acrylic brush. Dip the brush into your glaze and *roll* it down the candlestick. Roll the brush only an inch or two and then use the 1″ soft sable brush to soften and shape the clouds. Do this from top to bottom and all around both candlesticks. Make some clouds bigger and others smaller, and be sure to get glaze into all the indentations.

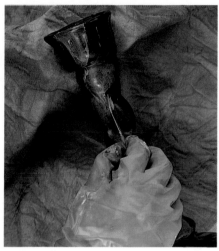

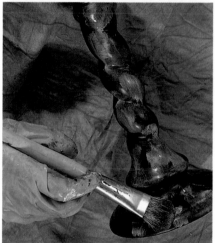

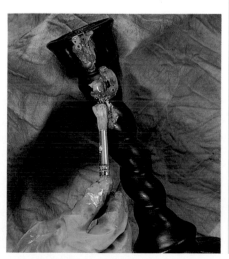

4 When you're finished, 50% of the black base coat should still be showing. Let dry for 4 hours.

5 Squeeze about ½" of yellow oxide into a container, and next to it, ½" of raw sienna. Have some water on the side. We're going to paint the veins. The veins in this marble follow the outlines of the clouds we just made and actually *link* them. Use a #4 acrylic brush and begin.

6 Vary the times you use yellow and a bit of water alone with times you mix the yellow with some sienna. Follow the outline of each cloud, and occasionally go *into* one. Make thin veins (with just the tip of your brush) and thicker ones (by applying pressure and flattening the tip). After you've made a few veins, use the 1″ sable brush to soften them.

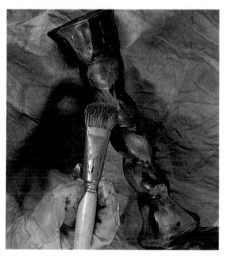

Also, make *areas* of color by flattening the brush and moving it left to right and up and down.

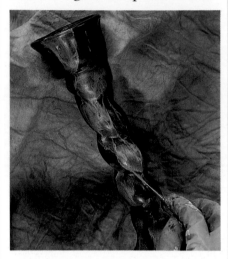

7 By the time you finish with both candlesticks, the first one will be dry enough for the final step: painting the white veins. (You can use the same brush—just wash it in some clean water.) The majority of these white veins should be in areas of black, but at times, *cross over* a yellow vein with a white one.

Tip: In marble, try never to cross over a line with another line of the same color. The eye accepts the cross over of one color with a different one, but accepts much less easily a crossover of the same color.

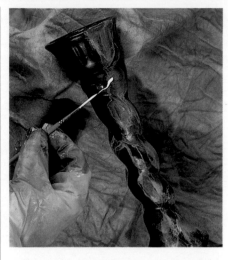

8 Make some of these veins very thin and some a bit thicker. Make some with straight paint and some with paint thinned with a bit of water. Do *not* use your sable brush to soften them.

9 When you're happy with the result, let the candlesticks dry for 30 minutes, then apply 2 coats of gloss water-base varnish with a 1″ acrylic brush. Let each coat dry for 4 hours.

10 By the way, I gave my friends the candlesticks with five different sets of candles. They were thrilled, and we inaugurated them at dinner the very same evening.

PLASTIC PICTURE FRAME

*t*HIS FRAME WAS ACTUALLY RESCUED FROM A GARBAGE HEAP BY MY FRIEND

DOMINIQUE, WHO KNEW THAT IT COULD BE MADE TO LOOK SENSATIONAL.

SINCE THE FRAME WAS ALREADY SPRAYED GOLD, GOLD SEEMED TO BE ITS DES-

TINY—BUT GOLD *LEAF* INSTEAD OF GOLD PAINT, AND *VARIEGATED* LEAF INSTEAD OF PLAIN.

RECIPE 7: PLASTIC PICTURE FRAME

Finish
Variegated Leaf

Time
Working time: just under 2 hours
Total time (including drying): just over 2½ hours

At a Glance
1. Clean the frame (10 minutes)
2. Apply shellac (10 minutes)
3. Let dry (30 minutes)
4. Apply gold size (30 minutes)
5. Let dry (15 minutes minimum)
6. Leaf (1 hour)

Materials
General
gloves, clean cotton rags, water, containers, stirrers, scissors, tack cloth, 4 jar tops to raise frame off work surface

Preparation
alcohol
clear, white shellac
2″ bristle brush

Gold Sizing
quick-drying size (water-base if you can find it)
1″ stiff bristle brush

Leafing
25 sheets of variegated leaf
1″ stiff bristle brush

Comments
• If you intend to use the frame to hold a mirror, remember that the mirror will reflect the inside part of the frame. Treat the inside with the same care as the more obvious places.

STEP BY STEP

1 Clean the frame with alcohol and a clean rag, use 4 jar tops to raise it off the work surface to get at the sides and edges. Apply clear shellac with a 2″ bristle brush (to make sure the frame will accept a coat of gold size).

2 Let the shellac dry for 30 minutes, remove the dust with a tack cloth, and you're ready for finishing.

3 Pour gold size into a container and apply it with a 1″ stiff bristle brush. Start with the carved portion on one side, then do the uncarved (this way you can be sure you've completed an entire side). Do the other side, the top and bottom, and the outside edges. In the carved areas, you'll have to "pounce in" the size gently (*pounce in* to get size into all the nooks and crannies, and *gently* to avoid forming bubbles). Remember, leaf does not stick to itself, so you need total coverage.

4 Let the gold size set up for a minimum of 15 minutes (2 hours if not water-base). When the size has achieved the right "tack," your index finger will not glide easily over the surface, but neither will it stick. Before you begin to leaf, change the newspaper on your work surface and remove your gloves.

5 Take a book of variegated leaf and cut the binding (the selvage) to free the individual sheets. In a carved frame like this, we will use about 25 sheets.

6 Start leafing with full sheets on the two long sides. Pick up a sheet between its two pieces of tissue paper. Let the front piece fall away and press the leaf into the side of the frame. Smooth it in place by rubbing your finger along the remaining tissue paper. The sheets will overlap onto the table. This is fine.

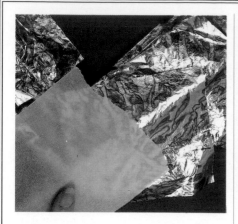

7 Leaf the top, bottom, and the carved sections in the middle.

8 Take a 1″ stiff bristle brush and begin to "pounce" away excess leaf. Start at the sides. The sections of leaf that overlapped onto the table will now come free. Pick these up with your brush and pounce them into the carving in the center, and the carving at the top. (Both these sections will need at least 2 layers of leaf in order to look right.) Pounce the skewings off the flat surfaces, pick them up, and pounce them into the carved sections.

As you proceed, start rubbing your brush into the surface as well as using it to pounce. Continue to pick up and use skewings in carved areas. Be patient. It's worth it. You will soon see the shape of the frame once again.

Rub the frame with your brush. This will "burnish" the gold color in the leaf and make the blue really "pop." Since the frame was sprayed gold to begin with, if you reveal some of the undercolor during pouncing, nothing is lost.

9 If you intend to leaf often, place all the remaining skewings into a box.

10 I decided not to varnish this frame. Varnish kills most of the color in varigated leaf. Variegated leaf contains a lot of copper and it *will* tarnish without protection. I chose the option of enjoying vibrant color and releafing when the frame becomes too discolored (from about 6 months to 2 years depending on your climate). I suggest you do the same.

SHOE HEELS AND TOES

*t*HE PLAIN TRUTH IS, YOU CAN APPLY THIS FINISH TO ALMOST ANYTHING AND PEOPLE WILL BE AMAZED—EITHER AMAZED AT HOW BEAUTIFUL THE OBJECT LOOKS, OR AMAZED AT *YOU* FOR EVEN *THINKING* OF STICKING TINY PIECES OF EGGSHELL EVERYWHERE. NO MATTER WHAT, THIS FINISH IS A REAL "WOW," AND YOU MIGHT BE ONE OF THE MANY WHO FIND IT ADDICTIVE.

RECIPE 8: SHOE HEELS AND TOES

Finish

· Eggshell

Time

Working time: about 4¼ hours
Total time (including drying): 3-5 days,
plus just under 17 hours

At a Glance

1. Prepare shells (3-5 days)
2. Shellac the heels and toes (5 minutes)
3. Let dry (30 minutes)
4. Apply shells (4 hours)
5. Varnish (5 minutes)
6. Let dry (4 hours)
7. Apply second varnish coat (5 minutes)
8. Let dry (4 hours)
9. Apply third varnish coat (5 minutes)
10. Let dry (4 hours)

Materials

General

gloves, clean cotton rags, containers

Preparation

3 eggs
Clorox bleach
white vinegar
1 plastic container

Shellacking

acrylic shellac
1″ poly brush

Finishing: Eggshell

white glue (like Elmer's)
#7 round acrylic brush
a piece of plastic wrap
a dressmaker's pin (any pin with a "head" so
you can handle it easily)
jar top

Varnishing

water-base varnish—satin
1″ poly brush

Comments and Tips

• Be prepared: Pieces of eggshell *will* fall off if you bang the shoe hard enough; this is not a permanent installation. But not to worry. If some falls off—put more on.

• The closer you're able to see an eggshell finish, the more precise it should be (that is, the smaller the pieces of shell and the more intricate the design—like what you would do on the back of a hand mirror, for example). With shoes like this, however, you can use larger pieces of shell.

• I am doing white shells on purple shoes, but if you want to use brown shells on white shoes, or whatever, go ahead.

STEP BY STEP

1 Crack open 3 eggs (and, since nothing should ever be wasted, make yourself a wonderful soufflé).

2 Soak the shells in Clorox bleach for 2 days. Eggshell is a membrane that dissolves in Clorox, so soaking makes them thinner (which is what we want). After 2 days, rinse the shells in cold water and let them dry for 24 hours. At this point, the shells should be brittle and thin enough to crack with an absolute minimum of pressure. If they aren't, soak them for another day, but this time in white vinegar (and again, rinse in cold water and let dry for 24 hours). White vinegar is more gentle than Clorox. Another day soaking in Clorox would disintegrate the shells almost entirely.

3 Use a 1″ poly brush to apply shellac to the heel and toe of each shoe. Let the shellac dry for 30 minutes and, as it's drying, separate (or break) your shells into 3 piles: small, medium, and large.

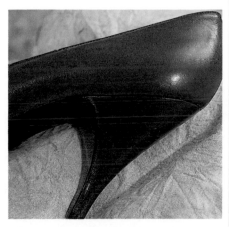

4 Doing an eggshell finish is a bit like doing a jigsaw puzzle: So sit down (it's always better to do this sitting), and choose your first piece. What we're going to do is fit pieces on the heel and toe.

5 Start with the heel. After the shellac is dry, pour some glue into a jar top. Dip a #7 round acrylic brush into the glue and coat about a 1″ square section.

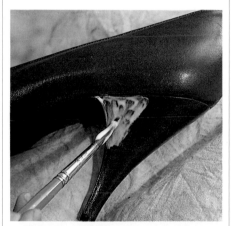

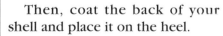

Then, coat the back of your shell and place it on the heel.

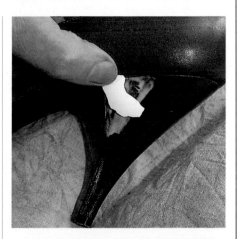

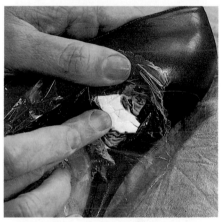

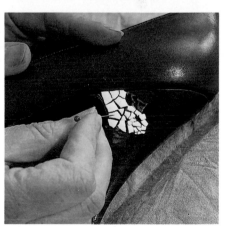

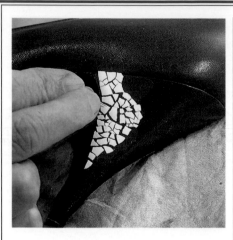

Cover the top of the shell entirely with a piece of plastic wrap and press gently. The shell will crack. Remove the plastic and use a pin to separate the pieces just enough so the purple shoe color is visible. If some pieces are still too big, apply pressure with the tip of the pin. A small amount will crack the shell so you can separate it.

Note: The amount of purple showing through the pieces of shell should be as consistent as possible. This is difficult to do, but it makes for a successful finish.

The real art here is finding (or making) the odd shapes and sizes you need as you move around the heels and toes. And I'll tell you something: You are going to know almost immediately if you love this finish or not. Many people find the precision it requires very relaxing. Others find it absolutely infuriating.

6 When you have finished with both heels, do the toes. As you can see in the final photo, I am graduating the pieces of shell from very close to wider and wider as I move from the front to the back. This is my choice; feel free to follow it or not.

7 As a final step, apply 3 coats of satin water-base varnish with a 1″ poly brush. We need 3 coats because the varnish has to fill all the spaces that separate the shell. Apply varnish and let dry for 4 hours . . . apply a second coat and let dry for 4 hours . . . and apply a third coat and let dry for 4 hours.

8 Now, look for the right occasion to wear the shoes, and anticipate the fun of answering the question that's sure to come over and over again: "What *is* that on your shoes?" This may be one of the few times that you can honestly say, "I'm walking on eggshells."

SALAD BOWL

*f*OR SOME REASON, I WAS GIVEN *THREE* SALAD BOWLS LAST HOLIDAY SEASON, SO I DECIDED TO TAKE THE SMALLEST AND LEAST INTERESTING AND DECORATE IT. THE FINISH I AM APPLYING TO THE INSIDE OF THE BOWL WILL MAKE IT IMPOSSIBLE TO USE FOR SALAD ANY LONGER, BUT IT WILL BE GREAT FOR DRY SNACKS (POPCORN, PRETZELS, NUTS, CHIPS) AND AS A SEASONAL CENTERPIECE. (IN THE SUMMER, PUT FRUIT IN IT . . . IN THE FALL, GOURDS AND INDIAN CORN . . . IN THE WINTER, CHRISTMAS ORNAMENTS . . . AND IN THE SPRING, WILDFLOWERS).

RECIPE 9: SALAD BOWL

Finish
    Inside: Spatter on Silver Leaf
    Outside: Art Nouveau Design

Time
    Working time: just under 4 hours
    Total time (including drying): about 4 1/2 days

At a Glance:
1. Clean the bowl (5 minutes)
2. Shellac (20 minutes)
3. Let dry (30 minutes)
4. Apply base coat (20 minutes)
5. Let dry (4 hours)
6. Apply second base coat (20 minutes)
7. Let dry (4 hours)
8. Apply gold size to inside bottom (5 minutes)
9. Let dry (15 minutes minimum)
10. Leaf bottom (10 minutes)
11. Apply gold size to sides (5 minutes)
12. Let dry (15 minutes minimum)
13. Leaf sides (20 minutes)
14. Porphyry (20 minutes)
15. Let dry (24 hours)
16. Apply design (1 hour)
17. Let dry (24 hours)
18. Varnish (20 minutes)
19. Let dry (24 hours)
20. Apply second varnish coat (20 minutes)
21. Let dry (24 hours)

Materials
General
    gloves, clean cotton rags, water, containers, stirrers, scissors, tack cloth, 4 jar tops to raise bowl off work surface
Preparation
    alcohol
    clear, white shellac
    1″ bristle brush
    flat latex paint—yellowish green (the color of green peppers)
    2″ poly brush

Gold Sizing
    quick-drying size (water-base if you can find it)
    2″ poly brush
Leafing
    10 sheets of aluminum leaf
    3″ rabbit hair brush
Finishing
    Japan colors:
- C.P. green—light
- C.P. green—medium
- raw umber
- Prussian Blue
- American vermillion

    commercial alkyd paint (8 oz. cans)—white and black
    4 spatter brushes or toothbrushes
    4 additional jar tops
    plastic teaspoons
    mineral spirits

Designing
Japan colors:
- Prussian blue
- lamp black
- a *new* long hair #6 artist sable brush
- mineral spirits

Varnishing
    oil-base varnish—matte
    2″ oxhair brush
    mineral spirits

Comments and Tips
• Spatter finishes tend to get *everywhere;* unless you have a very large work area, tape up newspaper to protect any surrounding walls.

• If you are not familiar with Art Nouveau design, you might want to look at a book or two on the subject.

• Whether you're following me or going off on your own, practice first. Art Nouveau lines have a particular flow, and you should get comfortable with how they twist, turn, and abruptly move from thin to thick. To practice making your design on a curved surface, tape a piece of paper to the outside of the bowl and, using paint and a brush, do some test runs.

STEP BY STEP

1 Clean the salad bowl with alcohol and a clean rag. Use 4 jar tops to raise it off the work surface so you can get at the bottom edges. Apply a coat of clear shellac with a 1″ bristle brush and let dry for 30 minutes.

2 You are going to apply 2 coats of yellowish green flat latex with a 2″ poly brush, but it's a bit tricky so try it this way: Paint the inside of the bowl without doing the top rim. Then flip the bowl over (so it's resting on the rim you didn't paint) and paint the outside. Let this coat dry for 4 hours. Now, apply a second coat, but this time don't paint the bottom. Paint the inside, the outside, and the top rim, and let dry for 4 hours (sitting on the dry bottom).

3 When the second coat is dry, you're ready for finishing.

4 With a 2″ poly brush, apply an even coat of gold size to the inside bottom of the bowl. Gold size is the adhesive to which the leaf sticks. You always apply gold size and leaf from the bottom of a piece to the top, because if you started leafing at the top, all the pieces that fall off as part of the process would land in unleafed places and stick in the size. When you leafed over them, the finish would be lumpy. Even though we're going to cover the leaf with porphyry, try for an equal coating of size. Evenly applied size prevents visible ridges under the leaf.

Don't underload your brush—you want to coat the entire surface. But don't overload it either; this will cause drips you have to touch up.

Quick-drying size is wonderful because it's ready to be leafed in no time, but it tends to form small bubbles. The more gentle you are when applying it, the fewer bubbles you will have. Both bubbles and drips can be seen in the final finish, so smooth them out now. Look for them especially around the seam where the sides of the bowl connect with the bottom.

Be sure to get size in this seam—using the front edge of the poly brush.

5 After you've finished applying the size, wait a minimum of 15 minutes for it to set up (or 2 hours if not using water-base). When the size has achieved the right "tack," your index finger will not glide easily over the surface, but neither will it stick.

6 Take a book of aluminum leaf and cut off the binding (the selvage) to free the individual sheets. We will use about 10 sheets on the inside of the bowl. Cut 3 of them in half and set aside.

7 Pick up a full sheet of leaf between its two pieces of tissue paper. Let the front piece fall away and press the leaf right into the middle of the bottom. Smooth the leaf in place by rubbing your finger along the back of the tissue paper.

Note: Even though aluminum leaf doesn't tarnish when handled, still use it with the tissue paper. This will help keep the leaf from tearing.

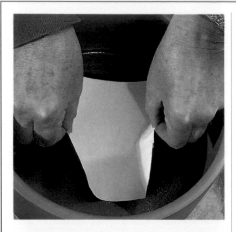

Use the half sheets to leaf the rest of the bottom. Leaf as close to the edges as possible all around. And it's okay if the leaf continues a short way up the sides. Cover as much area as you can, and don't worry about missed places—you will come back at the end to touch up. Don't rush. Leafing takes patience, but it's not difficult.

8 When you have leafed the bottom, take a 3″ rabbit hair brush and gently begin to smooth the areas where two leaves have overlapped. Brush in the direction of the overlap. (If you don't, you might tear the leaf.) This step smoothes the seams, joins them, and rubs off excess leaf.

The excess pieces (skewings) can be picked up with your brush and placed wherever you need them. As long as there is gold size on the bottom of the bowl, you can use almost all the skewings for touch-up.

9 When the bottom has been smoothed, clean the skewings off the surface and place them in a separate box. Finally, use a clean rag to do a final cleanup on the sides of the bowl.

10 Apply an even coat of gold size to the sides. Start at the top of the inside edge (that is, not on the top rim itself) and work your way down and around to the already leafed bottom. Try to avoid the bottom seam as much as you can.

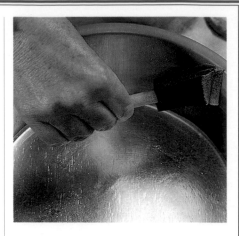

11 Wait a minimum of 15 minutes for the size to set up (or 2 hours if not using water-base).

12 Use full sheets of leaf and overlap them slightly as you move around the curves. Smooth the sheets by rubbing along the back of the tissue paper. The sheets will very likely tear as you smooth them into the size. This is because of the curve in the bowl. But don't worry about it, we will come back and use skewings to fill in the tears (or half sheets if the tears are very large).

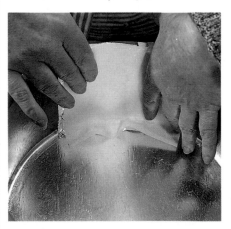

13 Now use the 3" rabbit hair brush as before to smooth in the direction of the overlaps. Use the brush to pick up and use skewings. If some size worked its way onto the top of the rim, there will probably now be leaf there as well. Just scratch it off with your fingernail, or use some base coat and carefully paint over it.

14 Put the remaining skewings in your skewings box, change the newspaper on your work surface, and get the paints ready for spattering.

15 In 4 jar tops, make 4 different glazes:

• ½ teaspoon of C.P. green—light, ⅛ teaspoon of raw umber (just the very tip of a spoon will do), 1½ teaspoons of white, and a drop of mineral spirits. Mix well.

• 2 teaspoons of straight black, and a drop of mineral spirits.

• ¼ teaspoon of Prussian blue, ¼ teaspoon of raw umber, 4 teaspoons of white, and a drop of mineral spirits. Mix well.

• ½ teaspoon of C.P. green—medium, the tip of a teaspoon of American vermillion, 2 teaspoons of white, and a drop of mineral spirits. Mix well.

To make life easy, place the paints and their individual brushes from right to left in the order below (this will help avoid mixing up brushes and colors when you start working). These are the coverages you want:

• Far right, C.P. green— light, 30% coverage

• Second from right, C.P. green—medium, 40% coverage

• Third from right, Prussian blue, 60% coverage

• Far left, black, 10% coverage

Note: Do keep in mind that spattering isn't science—it's *art*. The proportions and percents I give are guidelines. After you get started, if you want something different, just adjust your paints accordingly.

16 Ready to start? Dip the tip of your first brush into the C.P. green—light, pat off excess paint on your newspaper, and spatter color into the bowl by pulling the bristles of the brush toward you. As paint begins to accumulate on your "spattering finger," wipe it off on your apron or work surface.

There is no need to wait between colors—just apply one on top of the other. Repeat the process with all 4 brushes and all 4 colors.

Tip: If you end up with a blob of paint instead of a spatter, use the edge of a tissue to suck it up like a sponge. After a minute or two, spatter the area again.

Note: Spattering these colors on silver leaf is very elegant, but it's also very subtle. If you think you'd like another color variation, mix ½ teaspoon of black with ½ teaspoon of C.P. green—light. Spatter this at random. Or, you just might want to spatter on more black.

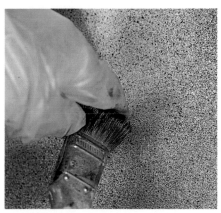

17 Let dry for 24 hours.

18 Now pencil in your design, both on the sides of the bowl and on the bottom. People tend to pick up bowls and turn them over, so we will decorate the bottom as well. Make the lines dark enough that you can see them, but don't worry about them—you will either paint over them or clean them off later.

19 In a container, mix 1½ teaspoons of Japan Prussian blue with ½ teaspoon of Japan lamp black.

20 Now sit down and get comfortable. This design requires practice and dexterity, but what it takes most of all is a "free hand." Start with the bottom (because it's easier to paint on a flat surface), take some paint on your brush, and let it flow. Get into a rhythm. Follow your pencil lines but don't be tied to them. If you're following a line but decide to go off somewhere else—go!

Note: I specified a new brush here because the "bounciness" of the sable will help you paint the design.

After you've painted the bottom, put your hand *in* the bowl and paint the sides.

Remember that you are working with oil paint, so if you don't like anything you've done, just carefully wipe it off with a rag and some mineral spirits.

21 When you're happy with the design, let the paint dry for 24 hours. Clean off any remaining pencil lines (with mineral spirits and a clean rag—just don't rub too hard) and apply 2 coats of matte oil-base varnish with a 2″ oxhair brush. Apply the varnish in the same way you applied the 2 base coats (review step 2 if you don't remember what you did). Let each coat dry for 24 hours.

SMALL METAL BOX

W HENEVER YOU FINISH A SMALL OBJECT WITH A BEAUTIFUL SHAPE (LIKE THIS BOX), CHOOSE A FINISH THAT CALLS THE EYE TO ITS LINES, CURVES, AND SURFACES. YOU DON'T WANT AN ELABORATE DECORATION; RATHER, YOU WANT SOMETHING JEWELLIKE THAT ASKS FOR ATTENTION IN A VERY SUBTLE WAY.

RECIPE 10: SMALL METAL BOX

Finish

Granulated Gold

Time

Working time: just over 1 hour
Total time (including drying): just over 9¼ hours

At a Glance:

1. Clean the box (5 minutes)
2. Apply base coat (10 minutes)
3. Let dry (2 hours)
4. Apply second base coat (10 minutes)
5. Let dry (2 hours)
6. Apply gold size with sand (10 minutes)
7. Let dry (15 minutes—minimum)
8. Leaf (20 minutes)
9. Varnish (10 minutes)
10. Let dry (4 hours)

Materials

General

gloves, clean cotton rags, water, containers, stirrers, scissors, tack cloth, a stack of books or a paint can to raise the box   to eye level

Preparation

alcohol
flat latex paint—red clay
1″ poly brush

Gold Sizing

quick-drying size (water-base if you can find it)
sand finish
1″ poly brush

Leafing

5 sheets of composition leaf (Dutch metal)
2″ stiff bristle brush

Varnishing

water-base varnish—gloss
1″ poly brush

Comments

• Keep sand finish away from the area where the lid of the box makes contact with the top rim. Depending on how often the box will be opened and closed, this is an area of wear that the finish can't stand up to. Use *plain* size here.

STEP BY STEP

1 Clean the box with alcohol and a clean rag. Situate yourself and/or the box so that it is at your eye level as you work.

2 Apply 2 coats of flat latex (red clay color) with a 1″ poly brush, and let each coat dry for 2 hours. After the second coat is dry, remove the dust with a tack cloth and you're ready for finishing.

3 Pour gold size into a container. Add sand finish a little at a time and stir. The more sand you put in, the more grain you'll have in the final finish. However, if globs and lumps form, you've put in too much. (If you tried to apply *this* mixture, the finish would just fall off.) If you *have* put in too much sand, pour out the size and try again, adding sand a little at a time.

Note: Feel free to experiment, but just be aware that a heavily grained finish will need at least 2 coats of leaf to look right.

4 Begin to apply gold size with your 1″ poly brush. Start in the rear of the box. Never start in front or right on top of an object. These are the two most visible display areas, so start in the back to get a feel for what you're doing.

5 Let the size set up for a minimum of 15 minutes before proceeding (2 hours if not water-base). Before you begin to leaf, change the newspaper on your work surface so that the only gold size around is what's already on the box. You'll also want to remove your gloves.

6 Cut the binding (the selvage) on a book of Dutch metal composition leaf. We will be using about 5 sheets to leaf this box.

7 Use full sheets and start working from the bottom. Pick up a sheet between its two pieces of rouge paper. Let the front piece fall away and press the leaf into the box. Smooth it in place by rubbing your finger along the back of the remaining rouge paper. Press all along the back so the leaf folds around the corners and edges of the box. Apply 1 sheet to each side and 1 sheet to the top. Leaf over the hinge at the back, and over the lid in the front and sides.

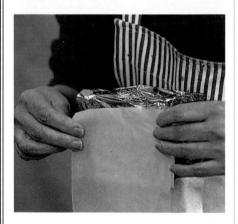

If your finish is heavily granulated, you might need a second coat of leaf. Or if you want a sandier finish, you will have to resize and releaf. (By the way, don't add more sand to the size, you will get a double dose just by using the mixture you already have).

9 Place all the remaining skewings in your skewings box if you intend to leaf often. Clean off your work surface.

10 Apply a coat of gloss water-base varnish with a 1″ poly brush. Let dry for 4 hours.

11 Do a final check of the box. Turn it upside down and look at the bottom. Does it look clean? (Should you paint it, perhaps?) What about the inside when you open it. Is it as nicely finished as the surface? There should be no mess and no drips anywhere. This is especially important on small objects like this box. They can be turned into jewels—but *all* their elements must be jewellike.

Rub your brush over the entire surface. This will "burnish" the finish and make it look more like real gold.

Note: Pay special attention to the hinges. Also, make sure you pounce back the separation between the lid and the box itself.

8 After the box is covered, take a 2″ stiff bristle brush and "pounce" the leaf into the surface. (Since the surface is granulated, the leaf cannot be smoothed on.) Pick up excess pieces of leaf (skewings) with your brush and pounce them back in. The more granulated your surface, the more skewings you will need. If you've missed places, apply more size and leaf again.

3
MEDIUM OBJECTS

VINYL RAINBOOTS

RAINBOOTS ARE DREARY BECAUSE WE WEAR THEM ON DREARY DAYS. SO LET'S USE SOME GLITTER AND MAKE *CHEERY* RAINBOOTS INSTEAD. THESE BOOTS WILL NOT ONLY CHEER *YOU* UP, BUT EVERYONE WHO SEES THEM WILL FEEL BETTER. AND DON'T BE SURPRISED IF PEOPLE STOP YOU ON THE STREET TO ASK WHERE YOU BOUGHT THEM (IT'S HAPPENED TO ME LOTS OF TIMES).

RECIPE 11: VINYL RAINBOOTS

Finish

Black Glitter

Time

Working time: just over 1 hour

Total time (including drying): just under 2 hours

At a Glance:

1. Clean the boots (5 minutes)
2. Apply gold size (30 minutes)
3. Let dry (15 minutes minimum)
4. Apply glitter (20 minutes)
5. Spray varnish (5 minutes)
6. Let dry (15 minutes)
7. Apply second varnish coat (5 minutes)
8. Let dry (15 minutes)

Materials

General

gloves, clean cotton rags, water, containers, stirrers, tack cloth

Finishing

quick-drying gold size (water-base if you can find it)

#2 round acrylic brush

black glitter (plus other colors if want)

large paint liner or top of box (big enough for a boot to lay flat)

plastic teaspoons

quick-drying spray varnish—matte

Comments and Tips

• Glitter will come off these boots as you wear them no matter *what* you do. But since it takes no time at all to apply more, just reglitter whenever you want.

• Don't bother putting glitter on the heels. Boot heels get so much wear and tear that glitter stands almost no chance of sticking there.

• I chose black glitter for these particular boots because I like the way it looks. You like red? Yellow? Combinations? Go for it!

STEP BY STEP

1 Clean the boots with water and a clean rag. And don't use gloves—they will only get in your way.

2 Lay the boots flat on your newspaper. Pour gold size into a container and using a #2 round acrylic brush, paint designs on the first boot. Paint your initials; circles, and circles within circles; paint geometric shapes, palm trees, or clouds with zigzag lightning bolts. Combine designs. Make them large or small, few or many. Have fun. The only limit is your imagination, and if you don't like something you've done, wipe off the size with water and a clean rag.

Tip: Be very generous with the gold size. Since the glitter has to stick to the surface of the boots, give it a solid base to hold onto.

Do the first side of both boots, then stand them up and paint designs on the feet.

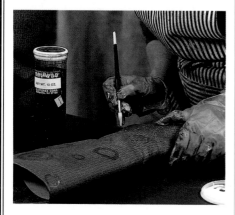

After that, put your arm in the first boot and hold it off the table so you can apply size to the second side. Do the other boot the same way.

3 When you're happy with the designs, let the gold size set up for a minimum of 15 minutes before proceeding (2 hours if not water-base).

4 Pour glitter into the paint liner or box top until the bottom is covered. Take the first boot, lay it down in the container, and *press* it into the glitter. Then pour glitter from the jar onto the boot. Make sure all the designs are covered. Do both sides, then stand the boot up and pour glitter over the foot. Do the second boot the same way.

Pour the remaining glitter back into its jar using a spoon or a funnel.

5 As a final step, use matte spray varnish to help keep the glitter in place. But do this outside, or with your arm stuck in the boot and held out a window. Ventilation is very important with this product. Go once over lightly on both boots. Let them dry for 15 minutes. Then apply a second coat and let dry for another 15 minutes.

6 If you've decided that there's no such thing as TOO MUCH glitter, you can let the first coat of spray varnish dry, then make additional designs with more gold size and a different color glitter . . . or two different colors . . . or . . .

7 If you're finished and there's no forecast for rain in the foreseeable future—simply call these "sun" boots, put them on, and take yourself outside for a walk!

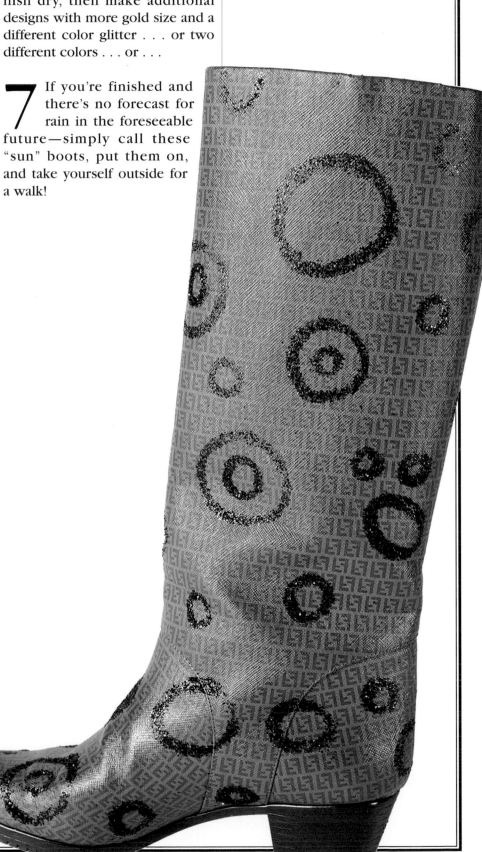

BATHROOM SET

(*Wastebasket, Tissue-Box Holder, and Tray*)

*t*HIS SET IS MADE OF PLASTIC COVERED WITH LINEN, WHICH AS YOU CAN SEE, SOMEONE TRIED TO PAINT BEFORE I FOUND IT. BATHROOM SETS CAN BE PRETTY USEFUL, BUT IT SEEMS THEY'RE ALWAYS UGLY. BY THE TIME *WE'RE* FINISHED, HOWEVER, THIS SET WILL STILL BE USEFUL—BUT UGLY NO LONGER.

RECIPE 12: BATHROOM SET

Finish
Sycamore with Ebony Inlay

Time
Working time: About 8½ hours
Total time (including drying): 4 days
and just under 18 hours

At a Glance
1. Clean the set (10 minutes)
2. Shellac (30 minutes)
3. Let dry (30 minutes)
4. Apply base coat (30 minutes)
5. Let dry (4 hours)
6. Apply second base coat (30 minutes)
7. Let dry (4 hours)
8. Draw and mask in design (30 minutes)
9. Apply first part of first half of design (1 hour)
10. Let dry (12 hours)
11. Apply second part of first half of design (1 hour)
12. Let dry (12 hours)
13. Apply first part of second half of design (1 hour)
14. Let dry (12 hours)
15. Apply second part of second half of design (1 hour)
16. Let dry (12 hours)
17. Mask in ebony lines (1 hour)
18. Paint ebony lines (1 hour)
19. Let dry (15 minutes)
20. Varnish (30 minutes)
21. Let dry (24 hours)

Materials
General
gloves, clean cotton rags, water, containers, stirrers, tack cloth, 12 jar tops to raise objects off work surface

Preparation
alcohol
clear, white shellac
1″ bristle brush
flat latex paint—light beige
2″ poly brush

Finishing
pencil and ruler
¼″ low-tack masking tape
painter's tape
interior stain—honey maple
acrylic paint—gloss black
two 2″ poly brushes
flat ¼″ synthetic artist brush
a piece of windshield wiper (or a rubber spatula)
single-edge razor blade

Varnishing
Polyshades (by Minwax)—Olde Maple
2″ poly brush

Comments and Tips
• If you don't want to follow my design, feel free to go off on your own—but keep it simple, keep your lines geometric, and pick a design that goes with the basic shape of your piece. It takes a good deal of time to mask lines properly in a project like this, so don't make it more difficult by trying for curves. All we basically want to do is contrast the wood grain of the sycamore with the black of the ebony.

• Before any new paint, varnish, or shellac step, use a tack cloth to remove accumulated dust.

STEP BY STEP

1 Clean the set with alcohol and a clean rag, prop the pieces on jar tops to raise them off the work surface, then apply clear shellac with a 1″ bristle brush. Let the shellac dry for 30 minutes, then apply 2 coats of light beige flat latex paint with a 2″ poly brush. Let each coat dry for 4 hours.

2 Use a pencil and a ruler to draw the design you want to do, then mask over the lines with ¼″ low-tack tape. Do this on all four sides (faces) of the wastebasket and on the other two pieces as well.

3 I decided to vary the direction of the sycamore grain. For example, the sycamore in the two outside areas and on the top of the wastebasket will go in the same direction, and the sycamore in the three middle areas won't. In order for this to happen, the center section has to be covered entirely with painter's tape. Do that now.

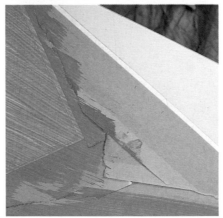

4 Open the can of honey maple stain. Stain separates into a liquid that floats on top, and "glop" that remains on the bottom. Pour three-quarters of the liquid into a separate container and use a stick to stir what remains. You want a heavy cream consistency, so if it's still too thick, pour in a bit more liquid until you get it.

5 With a 2″ poly brush, paint the unmasked areas on one face of the basket. Paint lengthwise—that is, move your brush in the direction of the length of the basket (see photo 00). The horizontal lines made by the poly brush will create the beginning of the sycamore, and the parallel grains we put in later do the rest. Also, while applying this coat, be sure to paint up to the edges of the tape. The poly brush will have a tendency to skip over these edges, so force it.

Wait 2 or 3 minutes for the stain to set up, remove your gloves, and pick up the piece of windshield wiper (or rubber spatula). We are going to make grains that are perpendicular to the lines created by the poly brush. To do this, hit the wiper into the stain. In order to make the grains, you actually have to *remove* paint, so hit hard enough to do so.

Make these parallel grains down the middle of the section you're working on, and make a few here and there on the edges. The grains on the edges suggest that this "piece of sycamore" was "cut" from a larger piece. Without the edge grains, the sycamore looks unnaturally even—artificial. After you're finished, remove the painter's tape.

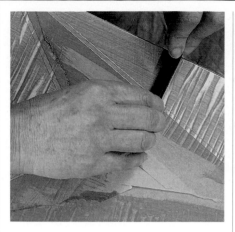

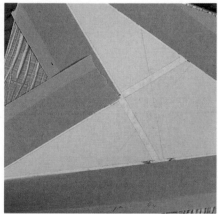

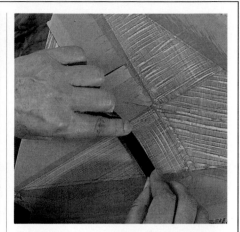

6 Do the same on the second face of the wastebasket (with the basket lying on a face that isn't painted). These two faces of the wastebasket constitute the "first part of the first half" of the design. Let dry for 12 hours.

7 The second part of the first half is the same as what you've just done—but on the two remaining faces of the basket. Don't forget to remove the painter's tape after you've completed each face, and let each dry for 12 hours.

8 For the first part of the *second* half of the design, cover all the sycamore you just created with painter's tape and apply stain into one of the center diamonds. Apply the stain in the *opposite* direction from what you did before. After allowing the stain to set up for 2 or 3 minutes, use your wiper blade perpendicular to the lines of the brush, as before.

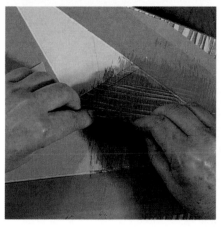

Next, paint the two long-side triangles, wait 2 or 3 minutes, and create sycamore grains parallel to the bottom line and moving upward. Remove the painter's tape, decorate a second face, remove the tape, and let dry for 12 hours.

9 Then do the other two sides the same way and let dry for 12 hours.

10 After the basket is dry, remove the original masking tape to reveal the lines of your design.

11 We now have another taping step to do. Use the ¼" tape and mask along the *outside* of your lines. This will protect the sycamore we've done from the "ebony" we're about to do. Be sure to push down (very gently) on the edges of the tape to prevent black paint from getting underneath.

12 When you're finished taping, use black acrylic paint right out of the tube and apply it with a flat ¼" synthetic artist brush. This acrylic will dry rapidly, so by the time you're finished with one face, you can move right on to another.

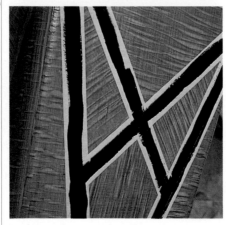

After you paint a face, slowly and carefully remove the tape. If you see that black paint has worked its way under the tape despite your precautions, carefully remove it with a cotton swab and a little water (or if it's dried, with a cotton swab and some alcohol).

13 Check all the ebony lines and edges. If anything looks ragged or unfinished, use some of the black acrylic and the artist's brush for touch-up. Paint the bottom and inside of the basket and the bottom of the tray. (Use the same black acrylic and one of the 2" polys.)

14 As a final step, use a 2" poly brush to apply a coat of Olde Maple Polyshades. This is an interesting product that combines stain and varnish. It's perfect here because it provides a nice, soft finishing color, plus the protection the set needs given where and how it will be used. Let the Polyshades dry for 24 hours.

Recipe 13

DISPLAY CASE

a DISPLAY CASE IS INTENDED TO PRESENT BEAUTIFUL OBJECTS, SO *IT* HAS TO BE BEAUTIFUL AS WELL. A CLASSICAL FINISH IS BEST IN INSTANCES LIKE THIS, AND I AM CHOOSING JAPANESE LACQUER BECAUSE OF ITS ELEGANCE AND SOPHISTICATION. THE FINISHED CASE HAS A DEFINITE ASIAN FEEL AND WOULD BE PERFECT FOR DISPLAYING SNUFF BOXES, OR SMALL FIGURINES. IT WOULD WORK JUST AS WELL FOR JEWELRY OR CRYSTAL.

RECIPE 13: DISPLAY CASE

Finish
Japanese Lacquer

Time
Working time: a little under 6 hours
Total time (including drying): a little over 11 days and 6 hours

At a Glance
1. Clean box (10 minutes)
2. Shellac (20 minutes)
3. Let dry (30 minutes)
4. Apply base coat (20 minutes)
5. Let dry (24 hours)
6. Apply second base coat (20 minutes)
7. Let dry (24 hours)
8. Paint (20 minutes)
9. Let dry (24 hours)
10. Paint second coat (20 minutes)
11. Let dry (24 hours)
12. Rub through (1 hour)
13. Antique (30 minutes)
14. Let dry (24 hours)
15. Varnish with red tint (20 minutes)
16. Let dry (24 hours)
17. Apply second coat varnish with red tint (20 minutes)
18. Let dry (24 hours)
19. Apply third coat varnish with red tint (20 minutes)
20. Let dry (24 hours)
21. Varnish (20 minutes)
22. Let dry (24 hours)
23. Apply second varnish coat (20 minutes)
24. Let dry (24 hours)
25. Apply third coat varnish (20 minutes)
26. Let dry (24 hours)
27. Buff with rotten stone (30 minutes)

Materials
General
gloves, clean cotton rags, containers, stirrers, jar, tack cloth, 4 jar tops to raise display case off the work surface
Preparation
alcohol

1″ masking tape
clear, white shellac
oil-base paint—flat black
two 2″ poly brushes
Painting
Japan color—sign craft red and bulletin red
oil-base paint—any white
mineral spirits
2″ soft bristle brush
plastic tablespoons
Rubbing Through
wet/dry sandpaper—a sheet of #400 and a sheet of #600
#0000 steel wool
Antiquing
Japan color—sign craft red and burnt umber
mineral spirits
oil-base varnish—gloss
spatter brush or toothbrush
pounce brush
plastic tablespoon and teaspoon
Varnishing
artist oil—cadmium red
oil-base varnish—gloss
1″ oxhair varnish brush
a sheet of #600 wet/dry sandpaper
mineral spirits
rotten stone
lemon oil
a piece of felt (optional)
single-edge razor blade

Comments and Tips
• Japanese lacquer is an "antiqued" finish that simulates the wearing-through of a surface color due to years of handling.

Look at the handles and hinges of your piece. If you think you might want to replace them, do it now rather than later.

• We're going to antique the case by spattering on color, which gets paint *everywhere*. If your work area is not large, tape some newspaper on any nearby walls.

• Before any shellac, paint, or varnish step, use a tack cloth to remove accumulated dust.

STEP BY STEP

1 Clean the case with alcohol and clean rags.

2 Apply masking tape. Mask around the glass in the doors to protect it from paint spills (on the outside and the inside). Remove the handles and use masking tape on the door hinges.

3 Before you start to paint, prop the case on 4 jar tops to get it an inch or two off the work surface. This will give you access to all the bottom edges. Take 2 paint stirrers and prop open the doors.

4 Apply a coat of clear, white shellac with a 2″ poly brush and let dry for 30 minutes. Apply oil-base flat black paint with another 2″ poly and let dry for 24 hours. Apply a second coat, let dry for 24 hours, and when the second coat is dry, you're ready for finishing.

5 In a container, mix 1 tablespoon of sign craft red, ½ tablespoon of bulletin red, ¼ tablespoon of white, and ½ tablespoon of mineral spirits. You want a mixture with the consistency of heavy cream. If your mixture is too liquid, add more paint, if it's too thick, add more mineral spirits.

Start with a 2″ soft bristle brush and cover the case with broad strokes. Since this is oil paint, you can paint in any direction you want, but the last time you go over it, paint in the direction of the grain. Use an easy, light hand and make sure you have 100% coverage.

Paint the doors, inside and out, the top, the sides, and the bottom. There is no need to paint the back of the case since it will be either hung on a wall or set on a table or shelf.

6 Pour your paint into a closed jar, wrap your brush in aluminum foil and put it in the freezer, and let the case dry for 24 hours. Then apply a second coat. (And no, the bristles on your brush won't freeze.) Let the second coat dry for another 24 hours and you're ready to "rub through."

Note: Since Japanese lacquer simulates a surface color worn off by years of handling, make a plan: Where would *this* piece have been handled? Clearly, the edges would have wear, but which ones and how much? And what about the flat surfaces? Once you've looked at the case logically, look at it artistically. Will enough areas be rubbed through? Too many? Make sure your plan is visually pleasing as well as logical.

7 Start with #400 wet/dry sandpaper. Cut a piece that fits your hand, moisten it, and rub the sandpaper back and forth in the direction of the grain. Keep the sandpaper moist and use a clean rag and water to wipe away excess so you can see how you're doing. Soon (depending on how heavily or lightly you use the sandpaper) you will begin to reveal some of the black base coat. At this point, switch to #600 sandpaper, or to the #0000 steel wool I am using. If you sand too much and reach bare wood, just paint in some black (use acrylic because it will dry quickly.)

What you want are areas that are totally black (where the finish has completely "worn off"), areas of black covered by a slight red film (where the finish has "worn off" somewhat), areas of black that are barely visible (where the finish has "worn off" hardly at all), and areas that are absolutely red. The case should be more than 70% totally red when you're finished. (Any less than 70% and the case will look more black than red.)

As I said before, the pattern of wear has to make logical *and* visual sense. This is an artistic judgment, and *you* are the artist. So, when you think the pattern looks good—it looks good.

8 The areas you have rubbed through now look old— but the rest of the box doesn't. So we have to "age" it a bit, and we'll do this with antiquing.

In a container large enough to accommodate a spatter brush, mix ¼ teaspoon of Japan sign craft red, 2 or 3 drops of Japan burnt umber, 1 teaspoon of mineral spirits, and 1 teaspoon of gloss oil-base varnish. Since you're going to spatter on the antiquing, you want a mixture with the consistency of thin cream (so adjust the proportions accordingly). If you want to adjust the color, vary the proportions of red and burnt umber. Experiment until you like how the color works with what's already on the case.

Dip the tip of your spatter brush into the antiquing mixture and choose a starting place. Hold the brush about 6″ from the case, pull the bristles toward you, and spatter away.

You want to spatter all over, but try to miss the black areas. Make small spatters first, and use a pounce brush to smooth and diffuse the flecks of color. Then, make bigger spatters. Pounce out some areas and not others. We don't want too "even" an effect.

Tip: An alternate method of spattering you might like is to hit the handle of your spatter brush on the handle of your pounce brush. This gives a different pattern than the old "finger in the bristle" method.

How much should you do? Well, you don't want to kill the red that's already there, you just want it to look as old as the rubbed-through sections.

9 After you're finished, let the case dry for 24 hours.

10 We're nearing the end, but by the time we get there you will probably be very tired of the word *varnish*. Remember, this is Japanese lacquer—and the finished product must have such a deep shine that people will want to dive into it and swim around. So, here's what to do:

Mix ¼ teaspoon of artist oil cadmium red, with 8 teaspoons of gloss oil-base varnish. Use a 1″ oxhair brush and apply an even coat all over the case. Let the varnish dry for 1 full day.

11 Then apply a second coat, letting it dry for a day.

12 Then apply a third coat and, yes, let that dry for a day as well. After the third coat, the exposed black areas will have begun to turn a bit red.

13 Now apply at least 3 more coats of varnish, but *without* the red, waiting 24 hours before applying each new color. All in all, there will be a *minimum* of 6 coats of varnish on the display case. After you have waited the final 24 hours, the end is in sight.

14 The finish on the case is now shiny all right, but it's shiny like a bowling alley—not shiny like Japanese lacquer. So use a piece of moistened wet/dry #600 sandpaper to remove the "plasticky" sheen. Give the case a complete once-over so the finish is smooth to the touch.

15 At this point you have your choice of 2 final steps. The first choice will make the case look great, but the second choice will make the case look **GREAT!** (Go for **GREAT!**)

Option 1: Mix 4 teaspoons of gloss oil-base varnish with 6 teaspoons of mineral spirits. Apply a thin, even coat and let dry for 24 hours. Or . . .

Option 2: Mix 4 teaspoons of rotten stone with lemon oil until you have a mixture the consistency of toothpaste. Take a piece of felt (I prefer to use my hands) and rub the mixture into the case. This step provides a very fine sanding *and* a polishing, so rub it in well. When you're finished, turn over the felt or use a clean cotton rag to buff the case.

16 Remove the masking tape from the glass (and the hardware), and use the razor blade for final clean up on the glass. You're finished. It was a good deal of work and you single-handedly supported the varnish industry for a time, but you have an object you can be very proud of.

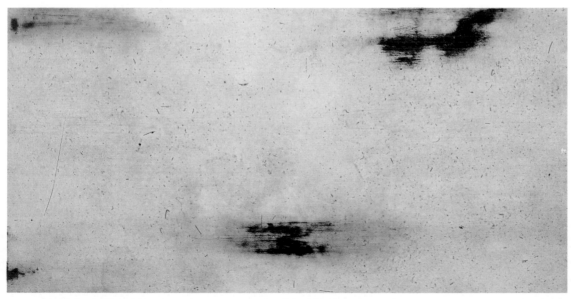

This is an example of Japanese Lacquer finish.

SET OF FOUR FOLDING TABLES

fOLDING TABLES LIKE THESE ARE *USED*, SO THE FINISH MUST BE PRACTI-
CAL. BUT THE TABLES ARE OFTEN USED AT PARTIES, SO THE FINISH
SHOULD BE FESTIVE AND FUN. I THOUGHT ABOUT THESE TABLES LIKE I
WOULD THINK ABOUT PLACE MATS AND DECIDED TO DO MALACHITE IN
FOUR COLORS. AND SINCE THE FORMICA TOPS WOULD BE MAKING SUCH AN
IMPRESSIVE STATEMENT, I DECIDED ON SOMETHING MORE SUBTLE FOR THE LEGS.

RECIPE 14: SET OF FOUR FOLDING TABLES

Finish

Malachite (Green, Blue, Burgundy, and Brown)

Time

Working time: just under 5 hours
Total time (including drying): about 6 days and 5½ hours

At a Glance

1. Clean the tables (20 minutes)
2. Apply bonding liquid to tops (12 minutes)
3. Let dry (30 minutes)
4. Apply base coat (20 minutes)
5. Let dry (24 hours)
6. Malachite (2 hours)
7. Let dry (48 hours)
8. Varnish (20 minutes)
9. Let dry (24 hours)
10. Apply second varnish coat (20 minutes)
11. Let dry (24 hours)
12. Finish legs (1 hour, 20 minutes)
13. Let dry (24 hours)

Materials

General

gloves, clean cotton rags, water, containers, stirrers, tack cloth

Preparation

alcohol
bonding liquid
oil paint—pale green
oil paint—pale blue
oil paint—pale pink
oil paint—beige
2" oxhair brush
mineral spirits

Finishing: Malachite

for the green malachite—artist oil permanent green; for the blue malachite—artist oil Prussian blue; for the burgundy malachite—artist oil Indian red; for the brown malachite—artist oil burnt umber

mineral spirits
¼" stiff bristle artist brush
2" poly brush
pounce brush
3 or 4 pieces of plastic (torn from a bag, or plastic wrap)
cardboard (the kind of material that's used in glossy postcards or catalog covers, must have *layers* when you tear it)
eraser (from the end of a pencil)

Varnishing

oil-base varnish—high gloss
2" oxhair brush

Finishing the Legs

oil-base varnish—gloss
bronze powder—gold
½" oxhair brush
plastic teaspoon

Comments and Tips

• In nature, malachite comes in one color only—green. So everyone will have a headstart in recognizing the green tabletop as malachite. The other three colors are fantasy colors. Of course, you can finish *all* the tops in green if you want.

• Malachite is a finish that depends on your level of skill and sense of design as much as on your ability to follow instructions. Look at the variety of shapes and ribbonlike lines in the photographs. Since you will be re-creating them on your tabletops, you might want to practice first. Mix paints in one of the colors, follow my instructions, and create the shapes on a *board* until you feel comfortable.

• We don't want to compete with the fabulous tops, but unless we do *something* with the legs, the project won't look complete. So we're going to add gold bronze powder to varnish, and finish the legs this way.

• Before any shellac, paint, or varnish step, it is advisable to use a tack cloth to remove accumulated dust.

STEP BY STEP

1 Clean the tabletops with cotton rags and alcohol, then use another rag to apply a coat of bonding liquid.

Note: Like most folding tables, these have Formica tops, and the bonding liquid will make sure the paint holds to the surface. If your tops are wood, however, use clear shellac instead. Both the bonding liquid and the shellac take 30 minutes to dry. After 30 minutes, use a 2″ oxhair brush to apply the 4 different base coat colors (oil paint in pale green, pale blue, pale pink, and beige). Let dry for 24 hours.

2 Start with the pale green top. Squeeze 1″ of artist oil permanent green into a container. Add about 2 drops of mineral spirits, then mix with a ¼″ stiff artist brush. You want a mixture with the consistency of custard, and without lumps.

When you have the custard consistency, add 2 more drops of mineral spirits and mix again. The final mixture should be like heavy cream.

3 With a 2″ poly brush, cover about 90% of the surface. Do this quickly and erratically. You are not looking for total, or smooth, coverage.

4 Crumple a piece of plastic so it has as many peaks and edges as possible. Pat the plastic onto the tabletop with light, short strokes. You are making a pattern called spinach malachite and it's a finish all by itself. You can actually stop here if you like the effect.

If not, take your pounce brush and gently "pounce" out the surface. Use uneven and random movements. Pounce out more paint in one area, and less in another. This pouncing is intended to create variety, so be sure areas with the spinach effect remain.

Tear the cardboard into 5 or 6 pieces of various sizes. It's important that you *tear* the cardboard rather than cut it. We want the ridges and uneven layers that come with tearing.

Take a piece and drag the torn edge through the paint. Make a ribbon by starting on one side of the table and continuing until you go off the other. Use different sizes of cardboard and make 3 or 4 ribbons of varying lengths and curviness. Refer to the photos, then make other malachite shapes: fans, scallops, chevrons. Use a round pencil eraser to make "nodules," the little round shapes in the middle of the fans. There are no rules. Experiment, and try for any effect you think you'll like.

This is a completely free process because if you don't like what you've done, simply apply more glaze, pounce it out, and start all over again. Take chances. No one will see your "mistakes" unless you want them to.

Practice. The more you do these various lines and shapes, the more comfortable you'll be. *You* decide when the design is complete.

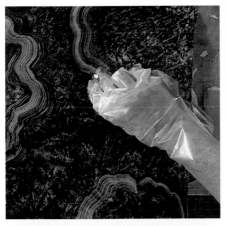

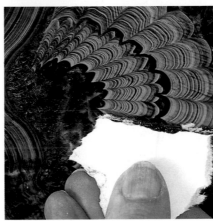

5 If you're going to finish the other tops in different colors, mix the paints and create the designs just as you did with the green. When you're through, let the tops dry for 48 hours. You are ready to varnish.

Tip: Before you varnish, touch each surface and make sure nothing comes off on your fingers. The tops must be *absolutely dry* or the varnish will remove the malachite. Use a high-gloss oil-base varnish and a 2″ oxhair brush. Let dry for 24 hours, then apply a second coat (and let *that* dry for 24 hours).

6 Now let's do the legs. Mix 3 teaspoons of high-gloss oil-base varnish with ½ teaspoon of gold bronze powder and stir well. These proportions appeal to *me*, but if you want a more pronounced gold color, just add more bronze powder. By the way, bronze powder has a tendency to settle to the bottom of varnish, so stir frequently as you work. Use a ½″ oxhair brush.

7 Be sure you paint the backs and all sides of the legs. You want full coverage, so walk around the table as you paint, or turn it frequently. You don't have to finish the underside of the table, but it should be clean. Paint it black, if necessary. Let dry for 24 hours.

MIRROR AND FRAME

LTHOUGH AN OBJET D'ART CAN MAKE A STATEMENT ALL ITS OWN, A FRAME AND MIRROR MUST FIT COMFORTABLY WITHIN ITS SUR-ROUNDINGS. A MIRROR IMMEDIATELY BECOMES A *PRESENCE*, SO ITS FRAME MUSTN'T FIGHT THE REST OF THE ROOM. THIS PARTICULAR FRAME BELONGS TO MY FRIEND DIANE, AND I CHOSE A FINISH AND COLOR COMBINATION THAT GO NICELY IN HER DEN. THIS COLOR COMBINATION, BY THE WAY, ALWAYS REMINDS ME OF ANCIENT POMPEII.

RECIPE 15: MIRROR AND FRAME

Finish
Pouncing and Striping

Time
Working time: about 2½ hours
Total time (including drying): about 20 hours

At a Glance
1. Mask the outline of the mirror (10 minutes)
2. Clean (5 minutes)
3. Apply base coat (20 minutes)
4. Let dry (2 hours)
5. Apply second base coat (20 minutes)
6. Let dry (2 hours)
7. Pounce (30 minutes)
8. Let dry (4 hours)
9. Varnish (20 minutes)
10. Let dry (4 hours)
11. Stripe (30 minutes)
12. Let dry (2 hours)
13. Varnish (15 minutes)
14. Let dry (4 hours)

Materials
General
gloves, clean cotton rags, water, containers, stirrers, tack cloth, 4 jar tops to raise the frame off the work surface

Preparation
masking tape
alcohol
flat latex paint—celadon green
2″ acrylic brush

Painting
flat latex paint—gray-green
water-base varnish—matte
2″ acrylic brush
pounce brush
plastic tablespoons

Varnishing
water-base varnish—matte
2″ poly brush

Striping
low-tack masking tape
flat latex paint—light red clay
water-base varnish—matte
#12 round acrylic brush
plastic teaspoons

Varnishing
water-base varnish—matte
2″ poly brush
single-edge razor blade

Comments and Tips
• If there is already a mirror (or picture) in your frame, take it out if you can. It's always easier to do a finish with nothing in the frame.
• It is a good idea to use a tack cloth to remove accumulated dust before any shellac, paint, or varnish step.

STEP BY STEP

1 If you could not remove the mirror or picture, mask it carefully all around to protect against paint, then clean the frame with alcohol and a cotton rag. To reach the edges and sides, prop the frame up on 4 jar tops.

2 Apply 2 coats of celadon green flat latex with a 2″ acrylic brush, and let each coat dry for 4 hours. When the last coat is dry, you're ready for finishing.

3 In a container, make a glaze with 3 tablespoons of gray-green flat latex, 3 tablespoons of matte water-base varnish, and 3 tablespoons of water. Mix it to the consistency of light cream.

4 With your 2″ acrylic brush, apply the glaze to small sections of the frame.

Use your pounce brush to pounce out the glaze. Acrylics dry very quickly. On a frame like this, for example, you cannot do a whole side at once. So when pouncing, do about 6 square inches at a time. Go fast and light. The effect you want is an overall "granulated" look, and you also want the celadon green base coat to show through.

First do the inside of the frame, then move to the outside. Move your head down to frame level to be sure glaze is pounced everywhere.

Note: If the frame holds a mirror, remember that the mirror will reflect the inside part of the frame. So treat the inside with the same care as the more obvious places. Don't fuss over the areas to be striped—they will be covered by a different color.

The pouncing action of this finish will cause excess paint to build up on your brush. After every three or four pounces, tap out the excess onto your newspaper.

5 Let the frame dry for 4 hours.

6 After the frame is dry, varnish it with matte water-base varnish using a 2″ poly brush. Let the varnish dry for 4 hours.

7 We are now going to highlight the 2 carved elements with a contrasting stripe. In order to protect the surfaces we want to stay green, mask them off with low-tack masking tape. (The tape is blue in the photos.) Low-tack tape is designed not to pull off an existing finish, but don't take any chances. Press down the edges to prevent the paint from getting underneath—just don't *press* down the edges. Get it?

8 In a container, pour 2 teaspoons of light red clay latex. Then add matte water-base varnish and water (a few drops at a time) until you have a mixture the consistency of heavy cream.

9 Use a #12 round acrylic brush to apply the color. You want full coverage, so make sure the paint gets into all the bumps and ridges.

10 After you've finished painting, gently peel off the masking tape (put it on just before painting and take if off immediately after). Don't even wait for the paint to dry.

11 Clean up any spills of red. Wipe gently and carefully with a rag and a little water. The red will come off easily because the surface is already varnished.

12 Let the paint dry for at least 2 hours, then varnish the entire frame again. Let dry for 4 hours.

13 If you were working with a mirror or picture still in the frame, remove the masking tape that protected it. Finally, scrape off any stray bits of paint with a single-edged razor blade. I had to give my creation away, but you can put yours right up on a wall!

MAGAZINE TABLE

tHIS IS AN ELEGANT SMALL PIECE WITH BEAUTIFUL LINES AND INTER-ESTING DETAILS. IT CAN EASILY BE USED FOR ITS ORIGINAL INTENT, BUT WOULD WORK JUST AS NICELY AS A NIGHT STAND OR SIDE TABLE. SINCE THE TABLE STARTED OUT AS WOOD (ALTHOUGH IT WAS PAINTED GOODNESS KNOWS HOW MANY TIMES) I DECIDED TO HIGHLIGHT ITS DIFFERENT ELE-MENTS WITH CONTRASTING WOOD FINISHES.

RECIPE 16: MAGAZINE TABLE

Finish

Light and Dark Wood Burl

Time

Working time: 4½ hours

Total time (including drying): about 3½ days

At a Glance

1. Clean the table (10 minutes)
2. Shellac (20 minutes)
3. Let dry (30 minutes)
4. Paint light areas (30 minutes)
5. Let dry (2 hours)
6. Paint dark areas (30 minutes)
7. Let dry (2 hours)
8. Apply light finish (1 hour)
9. Let dry (12 hours)
10. Apply dark finish (1 hour)
11. Let dry (12 hours)
12. Apply varnish (30 minutes)
13. Let dry (24 hours)
14. Apply second varnish coat (30 minutes)
15. Let dry (24 hours)

Materials

General

gloves, clean cotton rags, water, containers, stirrers, tack cloth, 4 jar tops to raise the table off the work surface

Preparation

alcohol

clear, white shellac

2″ bristle brush

flat latex paint—beige

flat latex paint—tan

2″ poly brush

low-tack masking tape

painter's tape

Finishing

interior stain—honey maple

interior stain—Philippine mahogany

artist oil—burnt umber

spatter brush or toothbrush

1″ poly brush

#3 artist sable brush

plastic

tissue paper

mineral spirits

Varnishing

oil-base varnish—satin

2″ oxhair brush

Comments and Tips

• Whenever you think about contrasting elements, first decide what overall impression you want the piece to make—light or dark. It's often not the size of the areas that dictates an overall impression, but rather the *importance* of the areas that are most visible. In this piece, I decided on a *light* impression with *dark* highlights.

• Be prepared to spend some time with painter's tape and low-tack masking tape. Contrasting elements are most visible in the line that separates the light from the dark areas. So no matter what piece you're working on, try to make the lines of separation perfect.

• Before any shellac, paint, or varnish step, it is advisable use a tack cloth to remove accumulated dust.

STEP BY STEP

1 Clean the table with alcohol and a clean rag. Use 4 jar tops to raise it off the work surface so you can get at the bottom edges. Apply a coat of clear shellac with a 2″ bristle brush and let dry for 30 minutes.

2 With a 2″ poly brush, apply beige latex to the areas you want to be light. Try to avoid the "dark" areas, but don't bother masking them off. (The tan paint will cover any mistakes.) Let the paint dry for 2 hours. Then cover the areas you just painted with painter's tape and apply the tan latex. After you've painted, remove the tape and let the piece dry for another 2 hours.

3 We'll start first with the light areas, so open the can of honey maple stain. Stain separates into a liquid that floats on top and "glop" that remains on the bottom. Pour half the liquid into a separate container and use a stick to stir what remains. You want a heavy cream consistency, so if its still too thick, pour in a bit more liquid.

4 Use a 1″ poly brush and apply the stain. Do it quickly and don't apply a *thin* coat either. We're going to *work* the stain, so we want a quantity of it on the surface.

Note: Be as careful as you can to keep the stain confined to the light areas, but don't go crazy because we'll clean up with mineral spirits and a rag when we're through.

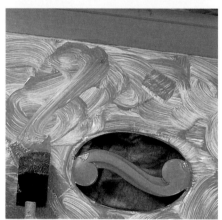

5 Form a piece of plastic into a rough cylinder shape and *roll* it through the stain. Burl has no direction, so roll it in left and right and up and down.

6 After rolling, crumple the cylinder into a rough ball and press it randomly into the surface.

7 Take more stain on your poly brush and randomly make the surface darker. Let your eye be your guide in terms of how much and where.

8 It's time for the tissue paper. Crumple it into a loose ball and tap it into the surface all around. This will create texture by *absorbing* some of the stain (as opposed to the plastic, which just moved it around).

98

9 Use the tips of your gloved fingers to make little "burls" here and there. Also use your thumb—it will make bigger burls. Do this all over the surface. Now take off your gloves and do the same thing with your *bare* fingers. These burls will have a different texture.

Tip: If you don't like what you're doing at any time, more stain and your poly brush will allow you to start all over again.

10 Squeeze out about 1″ of artist oil burnt umber on your newspaper. Dip just the tip of your toothbrush into it and spatter on some color. Find a starting place and pull the bristles toward you. This will spatter color in a random way. Wipe off any paint that accumulates on your "spatter finger" on your apron. Spatter color where it pleases you, but on no more than 5% of the surface.

11 When you're through, clean the lines that separate the contrasting colors with mineral spirits and a clean rag. Let dry for 12 hours.

12 After the light areas are completely dry, mask them off with painter's tape and low-tack masking tape (painter's tape on the flat surfaces and low-tack on the rest). Take all the time you need to do this properly.

13 Use the Philippine mahogany stain and follow all the same steps you did with the honey maple.

14 When you have applied stain to the entire dark area, squeeze about 1″ of artist oil burnt umber into a container. Dip a 1″ poly brush directly into the color and with the very end of the brush, *slash* burnt umber into about 25% of the surface. This will make the finish darker, and the stain already there will help diffuse and spread the additional color.

15 Use the plastic, the tissue paper, and your fingers as before. Depending on your piece, you may need to use a #3 artist sable brush to get glaze into all the nooks and crannies.

16 Spatter with burnt umber.

17 Take off the masking tape and clean up with mineral spirits and a clean rag. Put your finger into the rag and follow all the lines that separate the light and dark areas to make them as clean as possible. You may want to touch up here and there with the #3 artist brush and dark stain.

18 Let dry for 12 hours and then apply 2 coats of satin oil-base varnish with a 2″ oxhair brush. Let each coat of varnish dry 24 hours.

This is an example of Burled Wood (Light and Dark) finish.

CHAIR

I FOUND THIS CHAIR ON THE STREET, IN THE MIDDLE OF A SOAK-
ING THREE-DAY RAIN. I TOOK IT HOME AND HAD TO LET IT SIT
FOR ALMOST A MONTH UNTIL IT DRIED FULLY. AS YOU MIGHT
IMAGINE, THE RAFFIA (THE RATTANLIKE MATERIAL OF THE SEAT)
WASN'T IN THE BEST OF SHAPE, SO I HAD TO CUT SOME OFF AND
REGLUE SOME OF THE REST. BOTH THE SHAPE OF THE CHAIR ITSELF AND THE
RAFFIA SEAT SAID "AMERICANA" TO ME, SO THAT'S THE DESIGN I CHOSE FOR IT.

RECIPE 17: CHAIR

Finish
Americana

Time
Working time: 5½ hours
Total time (including drying): about 2 days

At a Glance
1. Clean the chair (15 minutes)
2. Shellac (30 minutes)
3. Let dry (30 minutes)
4. Apply base coat (30 minutes)
5. Let dry (4 hours)
6. Apply second base coat (30 minutes)
7. Let dry (4 hours)
8. Decorated horizontal sections (1 hour)
9. Let dry (15 minutes)
10. Varnish (30 minutes)
11. Let dry (4 hours)
12. Decorated vertical sections (1 hour)
13. Let dry (15 minutes)
14. Varnish (30 minutes)
15. Let dry (4 hours)
16. Paint seat (15 minutes)
17. Let dry (30 minutes)
18. Varnish (30 minutes)
19. Let dry (4 hours)

Materials
General
gloves, clean cotton rags, water, containers, stirrers, tack cloth

Preparation
masking tape
alcohol
clear, white shellac
1″ bristle brush
flat latex paint—pale yellow
2″ poly brush

Finishing
cider vinegar
dry pigment—terre verte
dry pigment—cobalt blue
dry pigment—ultramarine purple
measuring cup
plastic tablespoon
3 containers large enough to hold at least a half cup of liquid

three 2″ poly brushes
sea sponge, feathers, corks, plastic wrap, corncobs, putty, a comb, modeling clay (almost anything with texture, see first comment, below)
water-base varnish—matte

Varnishing
water-base varnish—matte
2″ poly brush

Comments and Tips
• What I am calling an "Americana" finish is more accurately called vinegar painting. Vinegar painting had its heyday in the 1800s in New England and the Pennsylvania Dutch country. It was primarily done by women and usually in the winter when everyone was forced inside for long stretches. Since their chairs, chests, and tables were most often made of inferior woods, the women developed materials and techniques to imitate the finer woods like bird's-eye maple, sycamore, and mahogany they couldn't get or couldn't afford. Then, they would often add designs on top of the wood they simulated.

They did all this with indigo, brown, and yellow pigments dug from the earth, and with green they would get from various molds. They would then combine these elements with vinegar (or beer) and make a gooey concoction they could work with. (The use of vinegar or beer rather than water gave body to the mixture and extended its drying time.) They had no brushes as such, so they used what came to hand: combs, rags, cork, corncobs, feathers, clay, and so on.

There are now serious collectors of these original pieces and they often sell at auction for equally serious money—prices in the $100,000 to $200,000 range are not at all uncommon.

I love vinegar painting because of this history. These were ordinary people simply trying to brighten their environment and be productive during the winter who turned out, in addition, to be brilliant and expressive artists.

• Before any new shellac, paint, or varnish step, use a tack cloth to remove accumulated dust.

STEP BY STEP

1 Use masking tape around the raffia seat to protect it, and then clean the chair with alcohol and a clean rag.

2 Apply a coat of clear shellac with a 1″ bristle brush and let dry for 30 minutes. Do *not* shellac the seat. Then apply 2 coats of flat pale yellow latex with a 2″ poly brush, letting each coat dry for 4 hours. (Do not *paint* the seat either.) Depending on the condition of your chair and the color you start with, you may not need 2 coats of yellow. After the first coat has dried, take a look and decide.

3 Here's what we're going to do. We're going to decorate all the horizontal surfaces first, then come back and do the vertical surfaces. (We'll do the seat last.) The steps will be: paint, let dry, shellac to protect what we've done, let dry, then repeat. The only slight complication is that we're going to *decorate* all the horizontal pieces, and *sponge* all the vertical ones. Got it?

4 Let's begin. We'll decorate the horizontal slats first. Prepare the 3 glazes:
• Pour ½ cup of cider vinegar into a container, add 3 tablespoons of terre verte dry pigment, and mix. The consistency you're looking for is light cream so add another tablespoon of pigment if you need more body.
• Pour ½ cup of cider vinegar into another container and add 3 tablespoons of cobalt blue. You want the same light cream consis-

tency so add another tablespoon of cobalt if needed.
• Make the same mixture with the ultramarine purple.

After you've made all 3 glazes, let them sit for 20 minutes. This allows the pigment to integrate fully with the vinegar. The mixture will actually thicken during this waiting period and work much better as a result.

Note: Before you begin the chair, remember that Americana is an unsophisticated, "primitive" form—so stay free and loose, and have fun. It's also one of the most forgiving finishes in the book because you can paint over it and start again *at any time*. Please experiment with color and materials and, unlike other projects where I suggest you practice beforehand, this time you can practice right on the piece itself. (Actually, the only problem is knowing when to stop. You may fall victim to "Hmmm, the feathered section looks great, but I wonder what would happen if I rolled a piece of cork across it.")

5 Apply some of the green mixture here and there on the first slat with a 2″ poly brush, then come back with some of the cobalt blue and some of the ultramarine purple (each with its own brushes).

Note: when you apply the colors, the surface might not want to accept them. Be insistent, *work* the colors in with the poly until you "season" the surface. This resistance will happen only when you apply paint the first time.

Use various materials on the

slats: feathers, cork, fingers, a piece of windshield wiper. Each of these materials yields a different pattern, so try them singly and in combination. As you can see from the photos, I even used the edge of a poly brush to get an interesting design.

Do all 3 of the slats in this manner, and don't forget their tops and bottoms. Now do the same on the round, horizontal leg braces.

6 When you're happy with all the horizontal surfaces, let the paint dry for 15 minutes. Apply a coat of matte water-base varnish with a 2″ poly brush. (Just wash out one of the brushes you've been painting with. After varnishing, wash it out again.) This will protect the areas you've done from any slips or mistakes you might make in the next steps. The varnish needs 4 hours to dry.

7 Sponge all the vertical sections. Make all 3 glazes again, just as you did before. Moisten a sea sponge and pick up a little of all the colors at the same time. Sponge them on, and then go over the glaze with your fingertips (wearing your

gloves, right?). Use your fingertips as much or as little as you like to get a design that pleases you. When you're happy with the result, use a clean rag to wipe off any paint that's gotten onto the horizontal surfaces (the varnish you applied previously will allow you to wipe it off easily). Let the paint dry for 15 minutes then apply a coat of varnish with a 2″ poly and let dry for 4 hours. (Again, just wash out a brush you've been painting with.)

8 Let's paint the seat. Make the glazes again and paint each of the 4 sections a slightly different mix of colors. Using a single 2″ poly brush and painting *in the direction* of the raffia, I painted one section blue, then added purple on top; one purple, with blue on top; one green, with blue on top; and the last blue, with green on top. (After I finished, I put a slash of purple highlight here and there for a final touch.)

9 After the seat has dried for 30 minutes, varnish the entire chair with a 2″ poly brush (seat included) and let it dry for 4 hours.

10 There you are. Have you created something that will be worth hundreds of thousands of dollars at auction one day? Probably not. But what you *have* done is made a beautiful object, had fun doing it, and continued a tradition that is *well* worth preserving.

VENETIAN MIRROR

*t*HIS MIRROR WAS IN SUCH AWFUL CONDITION THAT IT WAS BEING THROWN OUT. WHAT LOOKS LIKE TORTOISESHELL IN THE "BEFORE" PICTURE IS ACTUALLY THE REMNANTS OF THE GLUE THAT HELD THE MIRROR. BY THE WAY, IT IS *ALMOST IMPOSSIBLE* TO REMOVE "MIRROR" GLUE. IT'S A THICK, BLACK GOO AND ALL YOU CAN DO IS SAND IT OFF. SO SAND I DID, AND I ALSO PULLED OUT GLASS FRAGMENTS ALL AROUND THE INSIDE. I REPAIRED LARGE HOLES WITH WOOD FILLER, SANDED THE WHOLE THING SMOOTH AND, IN FACT, SPENT MORE TIME *PREPARING* THE PIECE THAN I DID FINISHING IT. BUT TAKE A LOOK AT THE "AFTER" PICTURE AND YOU'LL SEE WHY I BOTHERED. THE MIRROR IS ABSOLUTELY STUNNING.

RECIPE 18: VENETIAN MIRROR

Finish

Venetian Red Tortoiseshell

Time

Working time: just under 3¼ hours

Total time (including drying): 9 ½ days

At a Glance

1. Shellac (15 minutes)
2. Let dry (30 minutes)
3. Apply base coat (15 minutes)
4. Let dry (4 hours)
5. Apply second base coat (15 minutes)
6. Let dry (4 hours)
7. Apply finish (40 minutes)
8. Let dry (48 hours)
9. Varnish (15 minutes)
10. Let dry (24 hours)
11. Apply second varnish coat (15 minutes)
12. Let dry (24 hours)
13. Apply third varnish coat (15 minutes)
14. Let dry (24 hours)
15. Apply fourth varnish coat (15 minutes)
16. Let dry (24 hours)
17. Apply fifth varnish coat (15 minutes)
18. Let dry (48 hours)
19. Sand (15 minutes)
20. Apply sixth varnish coat (15 minutes)
21. Let dry (24 hours)

Materials

General

gloves, clean cotton rags, water, containers, stirrers, tack cloth, 4 jar tops to raise mirror off the work surface

Preparation

clear, white shellac

1″ bristle brush

flat latex paint—white

universal tint—Venetian red

2″ poly brush

Finishing

artist oil—alizarin crimson

artist oil—burnt umber

artist oil—black (optional)

oil-base varnish—gloss

mineral spirits

small, stiff artist brush

two 1″ oxhair brushes

2″ badger brush

pounce brush or toothbrush

1″ bristle spatter brush

plastic teaspoon

Varnishing

oil-base varnish—gloss

2″ oxhair brush

#600 wet/dry sandpaper (optional)

Comments and Tips

• If you are working on a mirror as well, remove it (if you can). It will make the project easier to do every step of the way. Also, the fabulous detailing on the top and bottom of *my* mirror (called "appliqué") screwed on and off. So I removed it and put it in a safe place for reinstallation later.

• Before any new shellac, paint, or varnish step, it's advisable to use a tack cloth to remove accumulated dust. This is especially true in a project like this where we are about to work very hard to achieve a smooth finish.

STEP BY STEP

1 Prop the mirror on jar tops to raise it off the work surface, then apply clear shellac with a 1″ bristle brush and let dry for 30 minutes. After the shellac is dry, prepare your base coat color. In a container, mix 12 teaspoons of white latex paint with 12 drops of Venetian red universal tint. You are looking for a rose color, so adjust the white and red accordingly. Apply 2 coats with a 2″ poly brush, letting each coat dry for 4 hours.

2 Mix 2″ of artist oil alizarin crimson with a few drops of gloss oil-base varnish. Only a small, stiff artist brush succeeds in integrating the paint with the varnish, so use one here. After you've mixed well, add a few drops of mineral spirits and mix again. You want the consistency of heavy cream.

In another container follow the same steps but use 2″ of burnt umber instead of the crimson.

3 You will apply both these glazes with 1″ oxhair brushes.

Apply burnt umber to 50% of the mirror, and crimson to 25%, leaving the last 25% with base coat showing. (Don't forget the sides.) Now, right away, use a 1″ oxhair brush to connect all the areas of color. The idea is that we don't want separate and disconnected "blotches" of color. (Use either of the 1″ oxhair brushes you just painted with; just wipe off the color with a clean rag.)

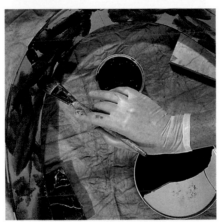

After this step, switch to a 2″ badger brush and go over all the areas you've just joined. Since badger hair is much softer than oxhair, this brush will actually *blend* the colors.

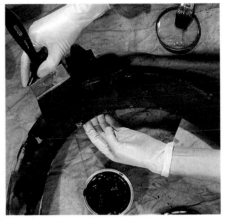

Use one of the 1″ oxhairs and come back with more burnt umber on top of the blended surface. Create tortoiseshell shapes on about 20% of the surface. Also, we are working with *color* as well as shape here. The finish will have more character when you come back with more burnt umber.

With the same brush, use crimson and make even more shapes—on an additional 10% of the surface. Avoid the burnt umber areas for the most part, but occasionally create new designs *into* and *on top* of them.

Note: I prefer the dark red finish this will create, but if you want it lighter, reverse the proportions and use 20% crimson and 10% burnt umber instead.

If you'd like, you can also use some oil-base black here and there to create highlights.

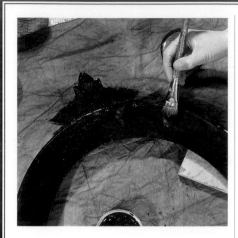

4 Use a 1″ round bristle brush to "pounce" the entire surface. We are pouncing here because the oxhair and badger brushes are too soft to guarantee a proper blending of all the colors. Pounce (push) color into all the edges and indentations (wiping excess paint on a clean rag). Pounce on the sides, then blend a final time with the 2″ badger brush.

Note: If you are working on a lightly carved piece, you will have to pounce after each step to be sure the colors get into all the nooks and crannies.

5 Now pour a little mineral spirits into a container, dip in just the end of your spatter brush, pull the bristles of the brush toward you, and spatter mineral spirits directly into the darkest areas of the mirror. The paint must still be wet when you do this so when the mineral spirits hits it, it will diffuse the color and create little circles. Spatter slowly and a little at a time. It takes about 20 seconds for the mineral spirits to have this effect, so don't be impatient, and don't blend these spatters.

6 When you're finished, let the mirror dry for 48 hours. (We've used varnish in all the steps thus far, so we'll give it 2 days to set up.)

Note: Venetian red tortoiseshell is one of those finishes that really lends itself to a "lacquer" feeling, so we're going to apply a minimum of 5 coats of varnish.

7 Apply gloss oil-base varnish with a 2″ oxhair brush, and let each coat dry for 24 hours. After the fifth coat, you can invest a bit more time if you want to make the mirror *really* special. Let the fifth coat dry for *48* hours (or if you live in a humid climate, for a third day). Then sand the frame with a piece of moistened #600 wet/dry sandpaper. Sand just hard enough to cut the gloss and make a finish that's smooth to the touch.

Note: We let the fifth coat dry for 2 days minimum to make sure this sanding wouldn't pull the varnish off the finish.

8 Finally, apply a *sixth* coat of varnish and let dry for 24 hours.

GINGER
JAR LAMPS

*t*HESE BEAUTIFUL AND AUTHENTIC CHINESE GINGER JAR LAMPS WILL BE A

PRESENCE IN ANY ROOM DUE TO THEIR LARGE SIZE, SO IT'S IMPORTANT

THAT THEY LOOK WONDERFUL. YOU CAN CONSIDER LAMPS LIKE THESE

EITHER OBJETS D'ART WHICH MAKE A STATEMENT ALL THEIR OWN, OR

INTEGRAL PARTS OF A ROOM WHICH HAVE TO FIT WITHIN A TOTAL DECOR. SINCE I

DECIDED TO MAKE THEM OBJETS D'ART, I CHOSE A *SPECTACULAR* FINISH.

109

RECIPE 19: GINGER JAR LAMPS

Finish
Base: Serpentine Marble
Body: Sienna Marble
Shade: Green Color Wash

Time
Working time: just about 6 hours
Total time (including drying): about 2 days and 22 hours

At a Glance
1. Clean the lamps (10 minutes)
2. Sand off peeling paint (30 minutes)
3. Mask off hardware (10 minutes)
4. Apply base coat (40 minutes)
5. Let dry (4 hours)
6. Apply second base coat if needed (40 minutes)
7. Let dry (4 hours)
8. Marbleize the bodies (2 hours)
9. Let dry (4 hours)
10. Varnish the bodies (20 minutes)
11. Let dry (24 hours)
12. Marbleize the bases (40 minutes
13. Let dry (4 hours)
14. Varnish the bases and the bodies (20 minutes)
15. Let dry (24 hours)
16. Color-wash the shades (30 minutes)

Materials

General
gloves, clean cotton rags, water, containers, stirrers, tack cloth, 8 jar tops to prop the lamps off the work surface

Preparation
alcohol
#280 sandpaper
low-tack masking tape
semigloss latex paint—linen white
2″ poly brush

Marbleizing the Bodies
semigloss latex paint—linen white
acrylic paint—raw sienna
acrylic paint—burnt sienna
acrylic paint—raw umber
water-base varnish—gloss
2″ poly brush
pounce brush
#10 round acrylic brush
#4 round acrylic brush
spatter brush or toothbrush

a piece of plastic
cotton swabs
4 containers (cat-food size)
plastic teaspoons

Varnishing the Bodies
oil-base varnish—gloss
2″ oxhair brush

Marbleizing the Bases
acrylic paint—white
acrylic paint—hunter green
water-base varnish—gloss
sea sponge
#4 acrylic brush
pounce brush
spatter brush or toothbrush
2″ poly brush
plastic teaspoons

Varnishing the Bases and the Bodies
oil-base varnish—gloss
2″ oxhair brush

Color-washing the shades
acrylic paint—hunter green
acrylic paint—white
3" poly brush

Comments and Tips
• Whenever you marbleize, you want to mix a bit more paint than you might actually need. This finish works best when you can feel "free" applying it, and you can't feel free if you're worried about paint. So overmix rather than undermix. The proportions in this recipe are just about right.

• Have *all* the colors mixed and ready before you begin. If you think you want to experiment with additional colors, have them ready as well. This will also help you feel free to do the finish.

• We are going to spatter on some color toward the end of this finish and spatter gets *everywhere*. So if your work area isn't large, tape up some newspaper on any walls and cover any favorite objects.

• There are entire books written on faux marble, so don't be discouraged at the beginning. The more marble you paint, the better you will get at it. And even if this is your very first time, the lamps *will* look like marble and you will have had a ball!

• Before any shellac, paint, or varnish step, use a tack cloth to remove accumulated dust.

STEP BY STEP

1 Clean the lamps with alcohol and clean rags. If any of the paint is peeling, use #280 sandpaper. Sand to the point where no other paint will flake off.

2 Mask off the bases of both lamps (the low-tack masking tape is blue in the photos). Then, remove all the hardware you can or want to and use masking tape to protect the rest.

Tip: Mask the electrical wire— all of it. This will take about 10 minutes and it's a worthwhile investment of time. It's very hard to clean paint spatters from electrical wire, and if you're a perfectionist, it's almost impossible. When the razor blade you're using to remove *that last little bit* slips and you slice the wire in two, you'll wish you had listened to me.

3 Prop the lamps on jar tops to raise them off the work surface so you can get at the bottom edges. Apply linen white semigloss latex with a 2″ poly brush. After the first coat is dry (in 4 hours), you'll be able to judge if the lamps need a second coat to cover the original color.

4 Prepare the 4 glazes in 4 separate containers.

• Mix 6 teaspoons of raw sienna, 6 teaspoons of gloss water-base varnish, and 6 teaspoons of water. This glaze should be the consistency of heavy cream.

• Mix 2 teaspoons of burnt sienna, 4 teaspoons of linen white, 4 teaspoons of gloss water-base varnish, and 2 teaspoons of water. This glaze should also be the consistency of heavy cream.

• Mix 2 teaspoons of linen white, 2 teaspoons of gloss water-base varnish, and 2 teaspoons of water. Again, mix to the consistency of heavy cream.

• Squeeze out ½″ of acrylic raw umber, and splash a little gloss water-base varnish next to it. Have some water nearby.

5 Soften a 2″ poly brush in water, then dip it into the raw sienna. Apply glaze in large drifts, get it on fast— *schmush* it on. Apply about 70% of the glaze in one direction (let's say on a diagonal from top right to bottom left) and 30% in the other direction. This ratio is important. The 30% highlights the main 70%, and helps the finish begin to say "marble."

After you apply about half the raw sienna, use your pounce brush to smooth and soften it. When thinking of "marble," most people think veins. But what really makes a marble finish work is what you're doing now: creating drifts. So in this first part of the finish, think: direction . . . flow . . . *drifts*.

Do both lamps up to this stage.

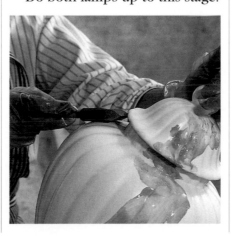

6 Now pick up some burnt sienna glaze with a #10 round acrylic brush and apply it in the same 70%–30% mix of directions. Put on the glaze, then use your pounce brush. Or crumple up a piece of plastic and pat it gently into the glaze. You can also use a crumpled rag, or even tissues. Patting almost anything with peaks and valleys into the glaze helps give the feeling of stone.

Tip: Make sure you work glaze under the rim of the ginger jar *covers*. Remember, lamps often sit on tables next to chairs and sofas, so people will tend to look up and under as well as straight on.

• What we've been doing so far

is making a "scumble." This is the base for the final marble finish. The scumble establishes the basic colors and the feeling of stone.

• Continue to work the glaze with the pounce brush or plastic until the result pleases you. There should still be about 10% of the base coat showing.

7 Use your #10 round acrylic brush and make big, gooey veins of linen white glaze. Roll the brush on its side through areas where the color is most intense. Vary the direction of the glaze as you apply it, sometimes going *with* the main direction and sometimes opposite it. Make a thick vein by applying more pressure on your brush, then make it thinner by applying less. Veins (which are actually concentrated drifts) appear randomly like this in nature.

Be careful to get glaze into the vertical ridges. Your brush will have the tendency to skip from peak to peak without going into the valleys. Don't let it.

Step back from the lamp. Does it say marble? Is it pretty? Is there enough contrast in the colors? Is the finish uneven enough to simulate something that occurs naturally?

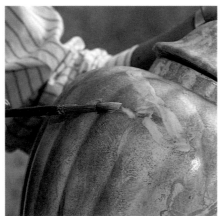

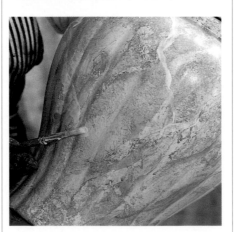

8 Make veins with your other 2 glazes for variety, going over and through what you've already done.

Tip: Never cross over a line with another line of the same color. One color crossing over a different color is acceptable to the eye, but a color crossing over the same color is not.

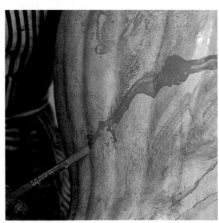

9 Now for the final veins. With a #4 round acrylic brush, take a bit of acrylic raw umber and a bit of varnish. Paint veins where the finish is boring and, surprisingly, where it's too busy. When you paint a dark vein in a busy area, the eye will go to *it* and make the area look simpler. These dark, intense lines will be *very* noticeable, however, so apply them sparingly—to no more than 10% of the surface.

Tips: You can also paint veins with a cotton swab. Pull out the cotton at the end and make a point. Dip the point into your glaze, then pull it gently over the surface. Let the swab do all the work. Apply a bit of pressure and you will get a thicker vein.

• Don't worry about where these veins begin or end. They can appear from nowhere and disappear into nowhere. Since they do so in nature—that's good enough for us.

• Whether you use a brush or a swab, don't pounce out the veins. And by the way, if you paint any raw umber veins you don't like, you can paint over them with linen white.

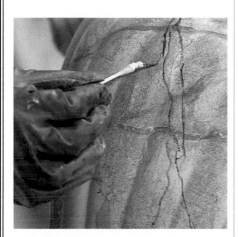

10 As a final touch, we will spatter on some linen white. Dip the tip of your spatter brush or toothbrush into the glaze and tap out the excess on your newspaper. Now look at the lamps. Where don't they say "marble" to you, or where do they look overworked? Point the brush at one of these places and pull the bristles toward you. This will spatter glaze onto the lamp. If the spatter turns into drips, lightly pounce them out with your pounce brush.

Use linen white to soften dark areas, then use the other colors to darken light ones. Spatter at random and when you're pleased with the result, let the lamps dry for a minimum of 4 hours.

11 Varnish both lamps. Apply a thin, even coat of gloss oil varnish with a 2″ oxhair brush, and let dry for 24 hours. Oil varnish holds better than water-base on ceramic.

12 For the two lamp bases, remove the low-tack masking tape that protected them—and protect what we just created by masking off 2 or 3 inches all around.

13 Make a glaze with 4 teaspoons of acrylic white paint, 4 teaspoons of gloss water-base varnish, and 4 teaspoons of water.

14 Moisten a sea sponge, dip it in glaze, tap off excess paint on your newspaper, and get started.

Sponge glaze here and there for a total of about 30% coverage. Use the sponge to get color into all the nooks and crannies.

Next, take a spatter brush, dip the tip into white glaze, hold the brush a few inches away from a base, and pull the bristles toward you. This will spatter white glaze in a pleasingly random way. Spatter all over.

15 Take your #4 acrylic brush and make veins in areas of black with the same white glaze. Roll the brush on its side and also use the tip. Make thick veins and thin ones, and be sure glaze gets into all the ridges and indentations. If a vein drips, blow on it to disperse the paint. Let dry 30 minutes.

Tip: You are about to work with a green glaze that can be seen only where there's white. (You'll see why in a minute.) Even though you don't want to cover the base *completely* with white, keep this fact in mind and make sure there's enough white.

16 Now make a glaze with 3 teaspoons of hunter green acrylic, 3 teaspoons of gloss water-base varnish, 3 teaspoons of water, and 1 teaspoon of the burnt sienna glaze from step 4. The mixture should be the consistency of medium cream.

17 Apply glaze to a section of the base with a #4 acrylic brush, then take a rag and "slap" or "swipe" it off. What you're doing is removing some of the green to reveal the white and black underneath. Apply glaze and "slap" it off around the entire base of the first lamp until you're pleased with the result. Then do the second base.

18 Next, do a few thin veins of white and/or a few spatters. If the veins look too fake, pounce them out to soften them.

19 Let both bases dry for 4 hours.

20 Remove the masking tape and, with a 2″ oxhair brush, apply gloss oil-base varnish to the bases, and (again) to the lamp bodies. This varnish will take 24 hours to dry.

21 In the meantime, let's do the shades. These shades are made of linen and are deeply pleated, so first remove all the dust and dirt you can (use a vacuum cleaner or Dustbuster).

22 Take the hunter green and linen white glazes you used on the bases and mix them 4 parts white with 1 part green. Then add water (a little at a time) to get the consistency of skim milk. I like this color, but you can make it darker or lighter just by adjusting the proportions of green to white.

23 A 3″ poly brush is the ideal shape to get paint into the pleats, so load up a brush and get at it. There is no secret to color-washing like this, other than finding the right angle so the paint doesn't drip.

24 When the lamps are dry, the shades will have been dry for quite a while. So plug the lamps in, screw in some bulbs, and see how you like the result.

4
LARGE OBJECTS

WOODEN STOOL

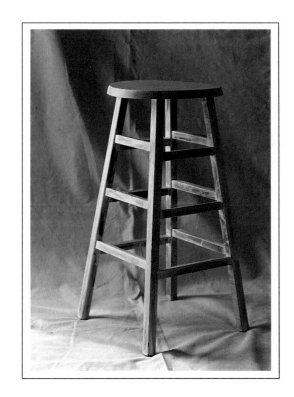

 WOODEN STOOL OFTEN LIVES IN A KITCHEN, CHILD'S ROOM, OR DEN—WHERE PEOPLE SIT ON IT AND PUT THEIR FEET ON THE RUNGS. IN ADDITION, A STOOL ALWAYS SEEMS TO BE CARRIED FROM PLACE TO PLACE, KNOCKING INTO WALLS, DOORS, AND EVERYONE'S KNEES. SO, THE FINISH WE CHOOSE FOR IT NOT ONLY HAS TO BE STURDY, IT HAS TO FIT IN ALMOST ANYWHERE.

RECIPE 20: WOODEN STOOL

Finish

Black and White Marble

Time

Working time: just over 2½ hours
Total time (including drying): just under
19 hours

At a Glance

1. Clean the stool (10 minutes)
2. Shellac (20 minutes)
3. Let dry (30 minutes)
4. Apply base coat (20 minutes)
5. Let dry (2 hours)
6. Apply second base coat (20 minutes)
7. Let dry (2 hours)
8. Paint veins (30 minutes)
9. Let dry (4 hours)
10. Varnish (20 minutes)
11. Let dry (4 hours)
12. Apply second varnish coat (20 minutes)
13. Let dry (4 hours)

Materials

General

gloves, clean cotton rags, water, containers,
stirrers, tack cloth

Preparation

alcohol
clear, white shellac
two 1″ poly brushes
flat latex paint—black

Finishing: Marble

acrylic paint—white titanium
water-base varnish—gloss
#6 acrylic brush

Varnishing

water-base varnish—gloss
1″ poly brush

Comments and Tips

• The colors of this stool were chosen because it was going into a black and white kitchen. However, when you see the final result, if you want more color, add some acrylic ocher or peach to the white, and paint-in additional veins.

• Before any shellac, paint, or varnish step, use a tack cloth to remove accumulated dust.

STEP BY STEP

1 Clean the stool with alcohol and a clean rag. Apply clear shellac with a 1″ poly brush (letting the shellac dry for 30 minutes), then apply 2 base coats of flat black latex with another 1″ poly. Let each coat dry for 2 hours.

2 On your newspaper, squeeze 1″ of white acrylic; splash some matte water-base varnish into a container; and have some water handy on the side.

3 Take a #6 acrylic brush and dip it into the paint, the varnish, and the water. Use the *side* of the brush—and paint a vein onto one of the legs. Make the vein thin and then a little thicker by holding the brush lightly and rolling it as you move. Do these veins sparingly all over the legs, and rub off any lines you don't like with water and a rag. Don't make any of the lines parallel. Parallel lines just don't look like marble, and besides, they're boring and ugly.

Vary the times you use paint, varnish, and water together with times you use paint and varnish only (without the water). This yields a variety of consistencies (from milk to heavy cream), which produces a variety of color intensities.

Move around the stool as you work. Remember that each leg (and leg brace) has 4 sides, so continue a line that you began in the front—to the back. Go around and over. Be free and let your brush wander. Keep your eye on the *whole* piece—don't overdo the veining, and try to balance the design in a way that pleases you.

4 Leave the top of the seat for last, when you're comfortable with the technique, and do the bottom of the seat only if you want to.

Note: When you think you're finished, turn the stool completely around at least two or three times to be sure you've covered all the sides and inside edges. Don't worry about smearing the paint, it will already be dry.

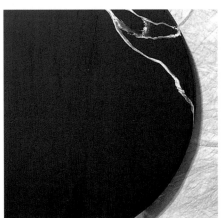

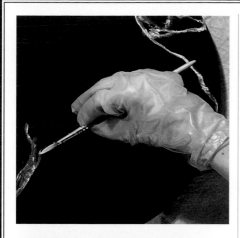

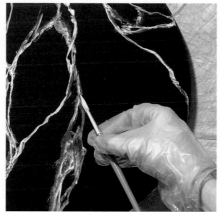

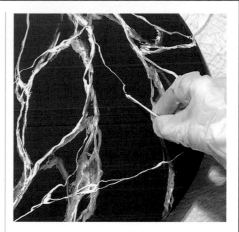

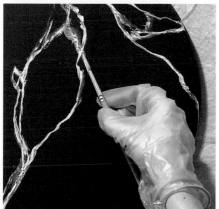

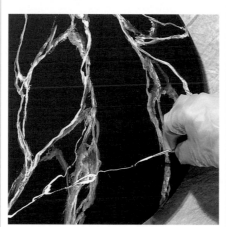

5 If you want more color, this is the time to mix ocher or peach into the white and paint additional veins.

6 Let the stool dry for 4 hours.

7 Apply a coat of gloss water-base varnish with a 1″ poly brush. After the first coat is dry (it will take 4 hours), apply a second and let *that* dry for 4 hours as well.

8 Then, take the stool into your kitchen, sit down, and take a look around. ("Hmmm, that table and those cabinets look a little boring. I have some base coat left and I've gotten pretty good at painting those veins, so maybe I'll just . . . ")

SMOKED PLASTIC CUBE

 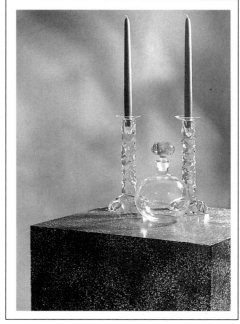

*t*HIS IS THE LARGEST OF THREE STACKING CUBES MADE OF SMOKED PLASTIC. LIKE ANY OBJECT THAT'S PART OF A SET, YOU CAN DO ALL THE PIECES IN THE SAME COLOR, OR CHOOSE A DIFFERENT COLOR FOR EACH. THIS CUBE WILL SIT IN A LIVING ROOM NEXT TO AN ABSOLUTELY GORGEOUS RED LEATHER SOFA. I THINK I'LL SEE HOW IT LOOKS THERE AND THEN DECIDE WHAT TO DO WITH THE OTHER TWO.

RECIPE 21: SMOKED PLASTIC CUBE

Finish

Granite (Reddish Purple)

Time

Working time: a little over 2½ hours
Total time (including drying): about
21 hours

At a Glance

1. Clean the cube (5 minutes)
2. Apply bonding liquid (15 minutes)
3. Let dry (30 minutes)
4. Apply base coat (15 minutes)
5. Let dry (2 hours)
6. Apply second base coat (15 minutes)
7. Let dry (2 hours)
8. Apply third base coat (15 minutes)
9. Let dry (2 hours)
10. Granite (1 hour minimum)
11. Let dry (4 hours)
12. Varnish (15 minutes)
13. Let dry (4 hours)
14. Apply second varnish coat (15 minutes)
15. Let dry (4 hours)

Materials

General

gloves, clean cotton rags, water, containers, stirrers, tack cloth, 4 jar tops to prop cube off work surface

Preparation

alcohol
bonding liquid
flat latex paint—magenta
3" poly brush

Painting

acrylic paint—Thio violet
acrylic paint—Payne's gray
latex paint—white
water-base varnish—gloss
3 sea sponges (1 for each color)
3 tray liners (or containers big enough to accommodate the sponge)
spatter brush or toothbrush

Varnishing

water-base varnish—gloss
universal tint—burnt umber
3" poly brush
measuring cup

Comments and Tips

• This will be a 3-color finish, and with the magenta base coat, we will actually have 4.

• We will apply the first color to the cube, then the second, and finally the third. This will give us a *definite* granite look. If we were to apply all three colors at the same time (that is, a little bit of this and a little bit of that), the colors would blend and the effect would be softer. You can experiment to see which effect you like better.

• If you want your granite lighter, use the white last; darker, use the gray last; more "colorful," use the violet last.

• We will spatter on color toward the end of this finish, and spatter gets everywhere. So protect your walls and favorite objects with newspapers.

• Use a tack cloth to remove accumulated dust before any shellac, paint, or varnish step.

STEP BY STEP

1 Clean the cube with alcohol and a clean rag. Then use 4 jar tops to raise it off the work surface to get at the bottom edges.

2 Apply a coat of bonding liquid with another rag. (This is to make sure the paint sticks to the plastic.) After it is dry (30 minutes), apply 3 coats of flat latex magenta with a 3" poly brush. Let each coat dry for 2 hours. After the last coat is dry, you're ready for finishing.

Note: If you have full coverage after only 2 base coats, stop there.

3 Use 3 separate containers to mix 3 tablespoons of each color (Thio violet, Payne's gray, and white), 3 tablespoons of gloss water-base varnish, and 1 tablespoon of water. You are looking for the consistency of heavy cream.

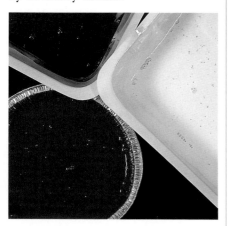

4 Start with the violet. Dip a sponge into the glaze and tap off the excess on your newspaper until you see a distinct pattern. (Every time you dip the sponge for more glaze, tap off the excess.) Apply color to the cube. Tap on the violet until you've covered about 70% of the surface. Be careful about drips and tap out any you see. Do all four sides and the top, then put the sponge aside.

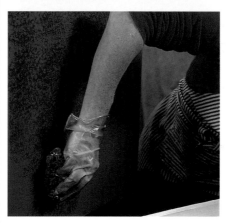

Apply the gray, using a second sponge the same way. This time, cover only about 30% of the cube. There is no need to avoid the first color.

Apply the white with a third sponge. You only want to cover about 20% of the cube this time. And again, don't worry about the first colors.

Note: Now step back and see how the cube looks. You can add more of any color just by tapping over what you've already done. You simply cannot go wrong because the colors are almost infinitely changeable. After you're pleased with the effect, there's a final touch that really gives the finish a granite feel. Patterns in natural granite would never be as even as those created by sponges, so we have to add some "unevenness."

5 Dip the end of a spatter brush or toothbrush into the white glaze. Point the toothbrush at the cube (anywhere) and pull the bristles toward you so paint spatters onto the surface. Do this in various places with the white, then clean the brush with water, dry it off, and do it again with the gray. Do it sparingly, however. We don't want to overdo the "unevenness" just as we didn't want to overdo the "evenness."

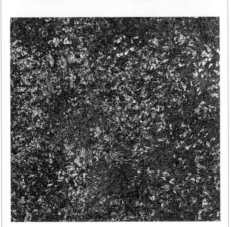

6 Let the cube dry for 4 hours.

7 The combination of the violet and magenta tends to be a little "sharp" to the eye. So we will kill this sharpness by "graying" the varnish with burnt umber tint. To 1 cup of gloss water-base varnish add 5 drops of burnt umber tint and stir. Apply the mixture with a 3" poly brush and let dry for 4 hours. Then, apply a second coat and let that dry for 4 hours as well.

BAMBOO FRAME

dECORATING THIS FRAME STARTED ME OFF IN THIS BUSINESS (ACTUALLY, *NOT* DECORATING IT IS PROBABLY WHAT STARTED ME OFF). MY FIRST TEACHER ASKED OUR CLASS TO BRING IN AN OBJECT TO DECORATE. I BROUGHT THIS FRAME AND TOLD HER I'D DECIDED TO DO A BAMBOO FINISH. SHE SAID, "MY DEAR, YOU WILL PROBABLY BE HAPPIER IF YOU CHOOSE SOMETHING MUCH SMALLER, AND MUCH, MUCH LESS COMPLICATED." I LISTENED TO HER AND THE FRAME SAT IN A CORNER OF MY STUDIO FOR THE LAST FIFTEEN YEARS. ITS TIME CAME AT LAST!

RECIPE 22: BAMBOO FRAME

Finish
Fantasy Bamboo: Male and Female

Time
Working time: just under 7 hours
Total time (including drying): $3^1/_2$ days

At a Glance
1. Clean the frame (20 minutes)
2. Apply the finish (2 hours each session; 3 sessions over 3 days)
3. Varnish (30 minutes)
4. Let dry (4 hours)

Materials
General
gloves, clean cotton rags, water, containers, stirrers, scissors, tack cloth, 4 jar tops to raise frame off work surface

Preparation
alcohol

Finishing
lacquer paint—gold
commercial alkyd paint—black
glazecoat
cardboard
1″ poly brush
#3 round synthetic artist brush
#6 round synthetic artist brush
mineral spirits
lacquer thinner
cotton swabs

Varnishing
water-base varnish—satin
1″ flat synthetic artist brush

Comments and Tips
• Bamboo is a finish that works well only if the object you're decorating has the shape of bamboo to begin with—either a piece like this which was made to simulate bamboo, or other (frames or legs) with rounded edges.

• Let's clear up the difference between male and female bamboo. Male bamboo grows in tight, parallel rings; while female bamboo has a stem instead of the rings. I'm doing fantasy bamboo (with gold dots and curlicues added), plus both male *and* female on the same piece. You can decide to do only one of them if you want, and female is by far the easier to do.

• I had already painted this piece terra-cotta years before, so I didn't have to do anything but remove the mirror, clean the frame, and get started. (If *your* frame has been painted something ghastly, however, choose a brown, tan, or terra-cotta color in flat latex and apply enough coats with a 2″ poly brush to get full coverage.)

• If you can, remove any mirror or picture from your frame before beginning.

• Before any new shellac, paint, or varnish step, it is advisable to use a tack cloth to remove accumulated dust.

STEP BY STEP

1 Prop the frame on 4 jar tops to raise it off your work surface and clean it with alcohol and a clean rag.

2 If you intend to do both male and female finishes, first make a plan for your frame, that is, what's going where. For example, I am making all the inside areas male and all the outside areas female. This balances the frame with a lighter feel on the outside and a more dense feel on the inside.

3 Let's start with the male bamboo. Use the #3 round synthetic artist brush and the gold lacquer and paint all the grooves/notches around the inside. This paint will take only about 10 minutes to dry, so by the time you're finished you can move right on to the next step.

4 Now, cut out a few 2″×2″ pieces of cardboard, then cut 6 or 7 notches of varying widths, each about ¼″ deep. To do this easily, just make ¼″ cuts in the cardboard, fold down alternating pieces, then snip them off.

These "combs" are about to save you a great deal of time.

5 In a container, mix 1 teaspoon of black paint and 1 teaspoon of glazecoat. This should mix to the consistency of *heavy,* heavy cream.

6 Apply a thickish coat with a 1″ poly brush and let it set up for about a minute. Then pull one of the combs through the paint, removing the glaze as you go. Wipe the excess on your newspaper and continue until you've completed a full section. (Refer to the photos to see what I mean.)

Tip: You will probably find it easier to start on the far surface and pull the comb toward you. After you're finished, let dry for 24 hours.

Cleanup Note: Use mineral spirits and a rag to clean up any slips with the black paint. You have to use lacquer thinner and a cotton swab, however, to clean up any slips with the gold. Be careful with lacquer thinner. Use a little at a time and do not rub very hard. Rub too hard and you'll go right through the gold to the base coat.

7 Let's begin to create the female design. First, paint all the outside grooves and notches with the #6 round synthetic artist brush and black paint. When you get to the smaller notches (in the latticework), switch to the #3.

8 Do all the ram's heads with black paint and the #3 artist brush. (You might want to draw a few of these with a pencil until you feel comfortable enough to do them freehand.) The stem part of the design is true to nature, but the ram's horns on both sides aren't (and obviously neither are the gold ovals and the black dots inside them. I told you this was *fantasy* bamboo, didn't I?).

Note: Don't feel as if you have to finish all the ram's horns in one session. Many people find this demanding and tiring, so don't push it. When it stops being fun, rest for a while.

9 When you *have* finished, however, let dry for 24 hours.

10 Let's do the ovals. Take some gold on your #3 artist brush, just *press* the brush into the frame, and lift. This will give you the desired shape. Not all of the dots will be the very same shape and size. To me, this is part of the charm of any hand-painted finish.

11 Let the ovals dry for 15 minutes, then go back and put a black dot into the center of each. (Clean the same #3 artist brush and use just the point.)

12 Let dry for 24 hours.

13 Apply a coat of matte water-base varnish with a 1″ flat synthetic artist brush and let dry for 24 hours. Then find the perfect spot to show off your wonderful frame.

VICTORIAN COFFEE TABLE

tHIS IS AN ACTUAL VICTORIAN HAND-ME-DOWN THAT WAS PAINTED OVER SO MANY TIMES, WHATEVER DETAIL IT ONCE HAD WAS TOTALLY OBSCURED. IN ADDITION IT TOOK MORE THAN IT'S FAIR SHARE OF NICKS, KNOCKS, AND BATTERING OVER THE YEARS. WHEN I SAW IT, I KNEW I HAD ONLY TWO CHOICES: EITHER STRIP IT DOWN TO BARE WOOD AND START ALL OVER AGAIN, OR CHOOSE A FINISH THAT TURNED ALL THE NEGATIVES INTO A POSITIVE. I CHOSE THE LATTER.

RECIPE 23: VICTORIAN COFFEE TABLE

Finish
Distressing

Time
Working time: about 5 hours
Total time (including drying): about 4 ½ days

At a Glance
1. Clean the table (10 minutes)
2. Shellac (30 minutes)
3. Let dry (1 hour)
4. Apply first color (30 minutes)
5. Let dry (2 hours)
6. Apply second color (30 minutes)
7. Let dry (2 hours)
8. Sand through (40 minutes)
9. Apply third color (30 minutes)
10. Let dry (2 hours)
11. Sand through (20 minutes)
12. Stripe edges (1 hour)
13. Let dry (24 hours)
14. Varnish table (30 minutes)
15. Let dry (24 hours)
16. Apply second varnish coat to top (10 minutes)
17. Let dry (24 hours)
18. Apply third varnish coat to top (10 minutes)
19. Let dry (24 hours)

Materials
General
gloves, clean cotton rags, water, containers, stirrers, tack cloth

Preparation
alcohol
clear, white shellac
3" bristle brush

Finish
latex paint—peach-pink
latex paint—pale yellow
latex paint—gray-yellow-green
acrylic paint—permanent Hooker's green hue
2" poly brush
#6 artist bristle brush
a sheet of #400 wet/dry sandpaper
#00 steel wool
mineral spirits

Varnish
oil-base varnish—matte
2" oxhair brush
butcher's wax (optional)

Comments and Tips
• Distressing is best suited for objects that aren't in very good shape to begin with. Distressing is a sanding-through process that starts with a top color and then reveals what's underneath. Therefore, if an object's been painted with different colors over the years, you'll see flashes of these colors in the finished product. Also, any imperfections the piece has will add character (so the more gouges and scratches the better).

• Before any new shellac, paint, or varnish step, use a tack cloth to remove accumulated dust. This is especially true in a project like this coffee table where we are about to work very hard to achieve a smooth finish.

STEP BY STEP

1 Clean the table with alcohol and clean rags then apply a coat of clear shellac with a 3" bristle brush. Let dry for 1 hour and you're ready for finishing.

2 Apply the peach-pink latex paint with a 2″ poly brush and let dry for 2 hours. Then apply a coat of the pale yellow with the same 2″ poly (just wash it out in water) and let that dry for 2 hours as well.

3 Moisten the #400 wet/dry sandpaper and begin to sand through. (Have some clean rags ready to remove the residue so you can see how you're doing.) Start on the outside of the top and work your way in. Keep sanding until you begin to see the first coat you applied (the peach-pink color). What you will also see are remnants of other coats of paint, all the nicks and scratches we talked about earlier, and in the case of my table, a lovely border design. In this step, we want to take off only about 20% of the surface color. Keep working on the top until you like the result, and then do the same on the sides and the legs.

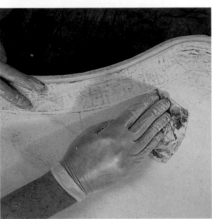

4 Clean off the table with another clean rag. Use a 2″ poly brush to apply a coat of the gray-yellow-green latex. Let dry for 2 hours.

5 Moisten the #400 wet/dry sandpaper and begin to sand through again (top, sides, and legs). This time, you want to take off 30% of the surface color. When you begin to reveal some of the colors underneath, switch to the #00 steel wool. Be careful to restrain yourself. The finish won't look right if you take off much more than the 30% I'm suggesting.

Note: You will probably have to do this finish a few times before you can be comfortable knowing how much is "too much" and what areas you want to distress. If this is your first try, however, follow my directions. But be fearless—it will look great.

8 With a 2" oxhair brush, varnish the entire table with a matte varnish and then apply 2 additional coats to the top only. It will take about 30 minutes to varnish the entire table and 10 minutes for each coat applied to the top. Allow 24 hours for drying between each coat.

9 If you'd like a special final touch, spread on a little butcher's wax and buff it with a clean rag.

6 Take some permanent Hooker's green hue (fabulous name, no?) right out of the tube with your #6 bristle artist brush and paint the edge all around the table. When you're finished, use a clean rag and immediately wipe off about 60% of it. The green should differentiate the edge from the rest of the table, but it shouldn't be too perfect—it should also look "distressed."

Tip: Use a little mineral spirits and a clean rag if you have to clean off any of the green. (By the way, I'm doing some highlights and detailing on the legs. If you intend to do the same, don't forget to wipe off about 60% of the color here as well.)

7 Let the green edging and detailing dry for 24 hours before varnishing.

RATTAN TABLE

*t*HERE IS PROBABLY MORE OLD RATTAN SITTING IN ATTICS, GARAGES, AND BASEMENTS THAN ANY OTHER KIND OF FURNITURE. THESE TABLES, CHAIRS, AND LOUNGES WERE INHERITED WHEN PEOPLE MOVED INTO NEW HOMES, WERE OCCASIONALLY BOUGHT AT GARAGE SALES, AND WERE EVEN RECEIVED AS GIFTS. IF *YOU* HAVE RATTAN, HERE'S FINALLY SOMETHING FUN TO DO WITH IT. THIS DESIGN EVEN COMES WITH A SUGGESTED DEBUT—YOUR NEXT FOURTH OF JULY CELEBRATION.

RECIPE 24: RATTAN TABLE

Finish

Pouncing (American Flag)

Time

Working time: about 4 hours
Total time (including drying): about 18 hours

At a Glance

1. Clean the table (10 minutes)
2. Apply base coat (30 minutes)
3. Let dry (2 hours)
4. Apply second base coat (30 minutes)
5. Let dry (2 hours)
6. Mask in stripes (10 minutes)
7. Apply stripes (30 minutes)
8. Mask in star field (5 minutes)
9. Paint star field background (5 minutes)
10. Let dry (30 minutes)
11. Apply star design (20 minutes)
12. Paint legs (30 minutes)
13. Let dry (2 hours)
14. Varnish (30 minutes)
15. Let dry (2 hours)
16. Apply second varnish coat to top (10 minutes)
17. Let dry (2 hours)
18. Apply third varnish coat to top (10 minutes)
19. Let dry (4 hours)

Materials

General

gloves, clean cotton rags, water, containers, stirrers, tack cloth, 4 jar tops to raise table off work surface

Preparation

alcohol
acrylic spray paint—matte white

Finishing

painter's tape
1″ masking tape
acrylic paint—naphthol crimson
acrylic paint—ultramarine
acrylic paint—titanium white
water-base varnish—satin
1″ stiff bristle brush
plastic tablespoon
hard, synthetic sponge (or a kitchen sponge that's gotten so stiff with use that you're just about to throw it out)
black marker (or pencil)
crafts knife
cotton swabs

Varnishing

water-base varnish—satin
1″ stiff bristle brush

Comments and Tips

• You have to be a little loose and easy about the concept of the American flag to enjoy this finish. Since we're doing it on rattan, the lines will never be perfectly straight, and there's probably no way you'll be able to fit all fifty stars.

• If some of the rattan is broken, cut it off or glue it back (with wood glue). Whatever you do, *don't* spend a lot of money sending the piece to a professional restorer.

• Remove accumulated dust with a tack cloth before any new shellac, paint, or varnish step.

STEP BY STEP

1 Clean the table with alcohol and a clean rag then spray it with matte white acrylic paint. It's much easier to get the overall coverage we need with spray paint because of all the "ins and outs" of the rattan. I needed 2 coats of white to cover the original color of my table, but take a look at yours after the first coat. If you're happy with the result, just skip the second. This acrylic spray paint will take 2 hours to dry.

Note: If you can spray the table outside—do so. If you can't, make sure your work area is well ventilated and wear a face mask (you can buy one at any hardware store). The less spray paint any of us inhale, the better. Also, spray paint has the tendency to get everywhere, so if you're spraying inside, tape up newspaper around your work space.

2 Use painter's tape to create the star field in the upper left corner (in the correct proportion for the size of the table you're working with). Then, put down lengths of 1″ masking tape to create the stripes.

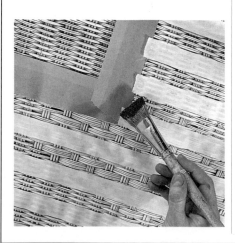

3 In a container, mix 4" of acrylic naphthol crimson with 1 tablespoon of satin water-base varnish. You want a mixture with the consistency of pudding so you can work it into all the indentations of the rattan. This is also why you'll use a 1″ stiff bristle brush. Get started, and as you work, you'll see that you're "pouncing" and pushing the paint *in* as much as painting it *on*.

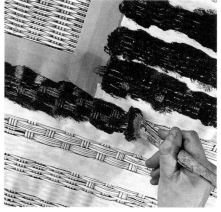

4 Remove the tape immediately after you've finished. If you were to let the paint dry completely, the tape would lift off the color you just applied. If you need to touch-up, use cotton swabs and water.

Wash and dry the bristle brush.

5 Apply painter's tape again to the outline of the star field. Squeeze out 2″ of acrylic ultramarine, and paint the blue background. You might find that the painter's tape won't stick, so just hold it down when you paint along its edge (and try not to get any of the blue under the tape). Apply the blue liberally (so that it enters all the grooves of the rattan and completely covers the white). Remove the tape, and let the paint dry for at least 30 minutes. Be sure the blue is dry before you move to the next step. If it isn't, it will mix with the white you're about to put on and this will *not* make you very happy.

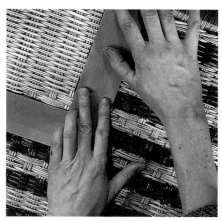

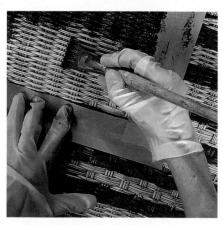

6 While the blue is drying, make a star "stamp." Use a black marker (or pencil) and draw a star on the sponge. (Make it a size that will work within your field.) Then, take the crafts knife and cut it out.

Tip: Wash off the black when you're finished, or cut *inside* the line. If you don't, the black might mix with the white. If you have a thin sponge, you might want to glue it onto a piece of wood so you can manipulate it easier.

Note: Before you actually apply the stars, plan what you're going to do. How many stars will the field take, and in what pattern?

7 Squeeze out 2" of white acrylic onto your newspaper. Dip the "stamp" you just made (unmoistened) into the paint, tap off the excess on your newspaper (until you see the pattern of the sponge—a few taps will do), and apply the stars. If you miscalculate or don't like what you've done, just repaint the blue and start again.

Note: You are not *painting* in this step—you are stamping, or printing. So just press the sponge down firmly, then remove it.

8 While the stars are drying, paint the legs. As with all pieces, think about it before you dive in. This is supposed to be a "fun piece." So what's fun for you? I decided to paint the legs and the solid crosspieces blue and leave the open areas of the crosspieces white (these open areas carry through the star motif). You can also carry through with more red (on the solid areas of the crosspieces, for example).

9 Let the paint dry for 2 hours.

10 Since this is a table, I am going to varnish the whole thing once, and only the top 2 more times. Use the 1" stiff bristle brush again. (You're going to have to "work" in the varnish just as you did the paint.) Water-base varnish takes 4 hours to dry completely, but only 2 hours if you're going to revarnish. So wait the 2 hours, varnish the top a second time, wait 2 hours, varnish the top a third time, and then wait 4 hours for the varnish to dry completely.

11 Of course, you don't *have* to wait to debut this table on the Fourth of July, but it would cause quite a stir if you did!

SCREEN

i ACQUIRED THIS SCREEN MANY YEARS AGO TO SEPARATE MY DRESSING AREA FROM THE BEDROOM. THE SCREEN WAS *GIVEN* TO ME BY THE OWNER OF A THRIFT SHOP WHO COULDN'T SELL IT FOR YEARS. BUT IT SAT IN MY STUDIO, AND SAT, AND SAT. AND MAYBE IT WOULD STILL BE SITTING THERE STILL IF IT WEREN'T FOR THIS BOOK. THE SCREEN IS MADE OF WOOD AND HAD CANVAS STRETCHED OVER IT WITH WALLPAPER PASTED ON TOP. THE END RESULT WAS PRETTY AWFUL. (NO WONDER NOBODY WOULD BUY IT.)

RECIPE 25: SCREEN

Finish

Glazing and Damask Stenciling

Time

Working time: just under 8¾ hours

Total time (including drying): under a day

At a Glance

1. Clean the screen (10 minutes)
2. Shellac (30 minutes)
3. Let dry (30 minutes)
4. Apply base coat to first side (30 minutes)
5. Apply base coat to reverse side (30 minutes)
6. Let dry (4 hours)
7. Apply glaze to first side (30 minutes)
8. Let dry (1 hour)
9. Apply glaze to reverse side (30 minutes)
10. Let dry (1 hour)
11. Stencil (3 hours)
12. Let dry (30 minutes)
13. Stencil reverse side (3 hours)
14. Let dry (30 minutes)

Materials

General

gloves, clean cotton rags, water, containers, stirrers, tack cloth

Preparation

alcohol

clear, white shellac

3" bristle brush

flat latex paint—light yellow-green

flat latex paint—light peach-pink

3" roller or poly brush

Finishing

acrylic paint—alizarin crimson

acrylic paint—burnt sienna

flat latex paint—yellow-green (two tones brighter than base coat)

water-base varnish—satin

bronze powder—gold

a sea sponge

3 containers big enough to accommodate the sponge

plastic tablespoons

piece of oaktag or plain wrapping paper

Stenciling

stencil

painter's tape

acrylic paint—iridescent gold, bronze, copper

water-base varnish—satin

a sea sponge

plastic teaspoons

Comments and Tips

• A standing screen like this is both useful and decorative. It's important to know in advance how you intend to use the screen because it will help you decide whether to decorate both sides or just the front. Not only am I decorating both sides, but I'm doing a different base color and stencil on each.

• Precut stencils can be bought in paint stores, artist's supply stores, and even some book stores. I'm using a 3-step stencil here. The different steps provide more detail, and each requires an additional application of paint.

• Sometimes the back of a stencil picks up paint from the surface. So always check the back before you place your stencil down in a new area. If you've had to clean paint off the back, be sure it's dry before going on to next steps. Stenciling is very easy, *but*, you must be precise, both in lining up and in cleaning up (no smudges allowed—neat edges only).

Stencil patterns are unlimited, and can provide almost any kind of "feel" you want. They allow you to be the artist and designer you've always wanted to be. If you can't draw, the stencil does it for you.

• I call this "Damask stenciling" because the stencil has the feel of damask fabric. If you are stenciling for the first time, choose a stencil that doesn't require many steps or complicated applications.

• If at all possible, take the hinges off the screen. It is *much* easier to work on separate panels.

• Before any new shellac, paint, or varnish step, use a tack cloth to remove accumulated dust.

STEP BY STEP

1 This screen needed quite a bit of preparation. I used wood filler to fill in more than a few holes and to even out many of the edges. I then had to sand it all smooth. (I hope your screen is in better shape.)

2 Wash the screen with alcohol and a clean rag, then apply one coat of clear shellac with a 3" bristle brush. Let dry for 30 minutes.

3 Apply the light yellow-green latex with a 3" roller or 3" poly brush. (The screen is big and the roller saves time.) Paint the panels while they lay flat on your work surface. Then, stand them upright and paint the reverse sides with the peach-pink. (This way, you don't have to wait 4 hours for the yellow-green to dry. You *do* however, have to allow 4 hours for this peach-pink side to dry.) Depending on the base color you're starting with, you might need a second coat on one or both sides. Take a look and apply it if you need it.

4 Into a container squeeze out an entire 2 oz. tube of permanent alizarin crimson, plus 2 tablespoons of satin water-base varnish, 2″ of burnt sienna, and a small sprinkling of gold bronze powder.

Note: You might not think you can even *see* the gold bronze powder in the glaze. But it's there, and it adds an undercurrent of richness to the completed screen.

5 Moisten the sea sponge, dip it into the glaze, tap off the excess on a piece of newspaper, and sponge color on the peach-pink side of your screen. You want full coverage. Let this dry for 1 hour.

Note: You "tap off" excess glaze until you see the pattern of the sponge on the newspaper. A few taps does the trick.

6 Into a second container, put 6 tablespoons of the two-tones-brighter yellow-green flat latex, 2 tablespoons of varnish, and another sprinkling of

gold bronze powder. Sponge this color onto the reverse side, with full coverage, and wait 1 hour for it to dry.

Note: Now, I want you to practice stenciling. Do it on a piece of oaktag, plain wrapping paper, or even newspaper. The time you invest practicing will be paid back when you start working on the screen. Practice two things: the technique of application (how much color to use and how to work it into the stencil) and the repetition of the design. For example, my design does not line up, that is, it doesn't go straight across from panel to panel. It must be staggered, or offset, and this takes practice to do properly.

7 Into a container, squeeze 6" of iridescent gold, 1" of iridescent bronze, ½" of iridescent copper, and 1 teaspoon of varnish. Mix well. I could have used straight gold, but I wanted the gold to be a bit more "brown" and antique-looking.

8 Tape down your stencil on the screen, moisten the sea sponge, dip it into the color, and tap off excess on a piece of newspaper. Sponge color onto the stencil. (By the way, I am going to apply this same stencil color to both sides of my screen.)

9 Allow about 15 minutes for the paint to dry and then proceed to the other stencil steps (if you have them).

Note: With the smaller pieces in my stencil, I usually just hold them down rather than taking the time to tape them.

Tip: As I said before, this damask stencil has to be *offset* from panel to panel rather than lined up straight across, so pay attention if your stencil has to be applied in the same way.

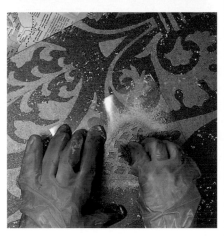

10 After the paint has dried for 30 minutes, repeat the stencil steps on the reverse side.

11 This screen needs no varnish step. There is already varnish in the glaze, and the screen will not be handled enough to require extra protection.

DESK

i BOUGHT THIS DESK AT A COUNTRY AUCTION IN NEW ENGLAND DURING A WEEKEND GETAWAY A FEW MONTHS AGO. IT WAS SITTING IN A BARN AND ALTHOUGH IT WAS VERY DIRTY AND PRETTY NICKED UP, I COULDN'T BELIEVE HOW GORGEOUS IT WAS. (SPENT $100. CAN YOU BELIEVE IT?) WHAT'S FUNNY IS THAT AS SOON AS I SAW THE DESK, I DIDN'T EVEN NOTICE IT'S ORIGINAL FINISH—ALL I SAW WAS SOMETHING ART DECO, LIKE THIS MACASSAR WITH IVORY INLAY.

RECIPE 26: DESK

Finish

Macassar with Ivory Inlay

Time

Working time: about 9½ hours
Total time (including drying): about 9 days

At a Glance

1. Clean the desk (1 hour)
2. Apply base coat (1 hour)
3. Let dry (8 hours)
4. Apply finish (2 hours)
5. Let dry (24 hours)
6. Draw inlay design (30 minutes)
7. Apply design (30 minutes)
8. Varnish (1 hour)
9. Let dry (24 hours)
10. Apply second varnish coat (1 hour)
11. Let dry (24 hours)
12. Varnish top only (10 minutes)
13. Let dry (24 hours)
14. Apply second varnish coat to top only (10 minutes)
15. Let dry (24 hours)
16. Apply third varnish coat to top only (10 minutes)
17. Let dry (2 days)
18. Sand smooth (1 hour)
19. Varnish (1 hour)
20. Let dry (24 hours)

Materials

General

gloves, clean cotton rags, water, containers, stirrers, scissors, tack cloth

Preparation

alcohol
#0000 steel wool
Polyshades (by Minwax)—Olde Maple, or flat latex paint in an orange-brown color)
2″ poly brush

Finishing

commercial alkyd paint—black
mineral spirits
glazecoat
1½″ oxhair brush
cardboard
cotton swabs
ruler
architect's tape—white matte, ⅟₃₂″
piece of white chalk
tracing paper
Saral paper—white
pencil
piece of acetate
a paper punch
acrylic paint—white
stiff #14 acrylic brush

Varnishing

oil-base varnish—gloss
2″ oxhair brush
bristle brush
#600 wet/dry sandpaper
mineral spirits
2 plastic tablespoons

Comments and Tips

• After the macassar finish is applied, I am going to do an ivory inlay design on top of it. If you'd like to copy mine, fine. If you'd care to design another, start thinking about it as you work. Macassar obviously makes quite a visual statement on its own, so choose a design that will complement rather than fight it.

• Before you begin working on any piece of furniture, remove all the hardware so you don't have to mask and fuss your way around it. When it's off is also a good time to evaluate the piece to see if the old hardware is still going to work with the *new* finish. I decided to replace the hardware on this desk. Take a look at the "before" picture and then at the "after" to see what I did. Do you want to do the same on your piece?

• Before any new shellac, paint, or varnish step, it is a good idea to use a tack cloth to remove accumulated dust. This is especially true in a project like this where we are about to work very hard to achieve a smooth finish.

STEP BY STEP

1 Clean the entire desk with alcohol and clean rags and then use the #0000 steel wool to remove any old varnish, wax, and dirt. Remove the hardware and take out all the drawers so you can work on them separately.

2 The wood on my desk was rather orange-brown to begin with (an elegant base color for macassar in my view) so I decided just to tint it with a coat of Polyshades Olde Maple. I like this product because it's stain and varnish combined and also because you can buy it in half pints. I applied it in the direction of the grain with a 2″ poly brush. Depending on the color of the wood *you're* starting out with, you might have to paint it with a flat latex orange-brown and 2″ poly. Start by painting the top of the desk (so you can pick up drips quickly). Then paint the sides (top down), the frame in front, the base, and then the insides. Let the first coat dry for 8 hours then see if it needs a second one. I didn't paint the back of the desk, but you'll want to if you intend to put your desk in the middle of a room.

3 During the desk's 8 hour drying time, cut 2 pieces of cardboard about 4" long and 2½″ wide (so you can hold them comfortably). Make them into "combs" by cutting notches into the short end of each piece. Vary the size of the notches from thick to thin but don't make them more than about ⅛″ long. If they're much longer, they'll be too flexible for their intended purpose. Refer to photo 00 to see what I'm talking about.

4 When the desk is dry, make a glaze with 8 tablespoons of black alkyd paint, 1 tablespoon of mineral spirits, and 2 tablespoons of glazecoat. Mix this to the consistency of heavy cream. (If you need more glaze, follow the same proportions.)

5 Apply the glaze with a 1½″ oxhair brush to the entire top of the desk. (For simplicity's sake, I'm working on a single drawer in the step-by-step photos.) Now, start at an end and pull one of the notched cardboard combs through the paint. Go all the way across and off the other side. (Wipe the excess paint on your newspaper.) Macassar wood grain is basically varying widths of parallel lines, and we're simulating this by using the cardboard to remove surface paint and reveal the color underneath. Sometimes the cardboard won't remove paint from the edges, so have some cotton swabs handy and use them where you have to.

Finish "graining" the top and then do the sides and all the drawers. Feel loose and free when doing this finish because you simply cannot go wrong. If you don't like what you've done, just rub it off with a clean rag and some mineral spirits, reglaze, and start all over again.

6 Let the finish dry for 24 hours.

7 Let's make the ivory inlay. Start with the straight lines. Measure where you want your lincs to go then lay down the architect's tape. Since the tape is very thin, it will stretch if you lift it off and try to lay it down again, so measure carefully and don't press it in place until you're sure of its position.

8 Now, take a piece of chalk and draw (freehand) the rest of the design (the two swirls) on the desk top. One of the great things about using chalk is that you can apply it and wipe it off endlessly. When you are pleased with what you've drawn, put a piece of tracing paper over the *half* of the design you prefer, and trace it.

9 Now, turn the tracing paper over and tape it down on the other side of the top. In a curved design like this, it's critical that both sides be identical—and this is where the Saral paper comes in. Saral paper serves the same function as carbon paper. Making sure that the chalk side is down, slide the Saral paper under the tracing paper. Go over the curved line with a pencil (using a bit of pressure), remove both the Saral paper and the tracing paper, and voilà! Identical designs on *both* sides of the desk top.

10 Cut out a 2″ square piece of the acetate sheet and punch out 2 holes, 1″ apart. You've just created a stencil that will make applying the ivory "dots" a snap.

11 Using white acrylic paint right out of the tube and your stiff #14 acrylic brush, paint the dots all around the curved lines. Paint the first two dots, then line up the stencil on one you've painted and paint the next. Line it up and paint the next, and do this all around the curves. Why paint only one new dot at a time? Why not make a stencil with five or six dots? Because we're painting dots around curves, and it's impossible to do more than one new one at a time. You will find, by the way, that the paint dries almost immc-diately. (If you'd like, you can also paint a dot where the straight lines intersect.) Just remember to wipe off chalk lines when you are finished.

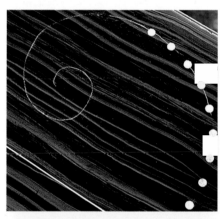

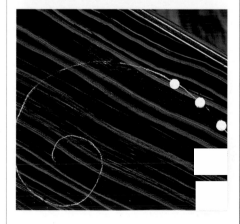

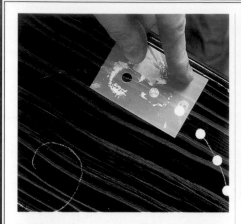

15 Mix 2 tablespoons of varnish and 2 table-spoons of mineral spirits. Apply a light coat to the top with an oxhair brush. By the way, we are cutting the varnish with mineral spirits to avoid a "plasticky" look and achieve a real lacquer feel.

16 Let this last coat of varnish dry for 24 hours and install the (new or old) hardware. You have created a showpiece!

13 After the second coat has dried for 24 hours, varnish the top (only the top) 3 more times, waiting 24 hours between coats. After you apply the third coat of varnish, let the desk sit for 2 days. For what we're about to do, the varnish has to be dry (and if you live in a humid climate, you should probably let it sit for a third day).

12 This desk is going to be beautiful enough to stop traffic, and the lacquer "feel" we're going to give it adds to the impact. Apply a coat of gloss oil-base varnish with a 2″ oxhair brush, let the varnish dry for 24 hours, and apply a second coat.

14 Moisten the #600 wet/dry sandpaper and sand until the top is smooth to the touch. Be sure to use a clean rag to remove all the residue as you work.

HEADBOARD

*t*HIS HEADBOARD BELONGED TO AN HONEST-TO-GOODNESS RUSSIAN COUNT. BUT AS IT WAS MOVED FROM HOUSE TO HOUSE AND COUNTRY TO COUNTRY OVER THE YEARS, IT FINALLY BECAME SO TATTERED THAT IT WOUND UP IN MY STUDIO. DESPITE ITS WOEFUL CONDITION, IT HAS A GREAT BAROQUE SHAPE AND A WONDERFUL ALL-AROUND BORDER OF SILVER LEAF. SINCE I WANTED TO BRING BACK ITS OLD GLAMOUR AND COMPLEMENT ITS UNMISTAK-ABLE QUALITY, I CHOSE A FANTASY OF SHAPES AND COLORS, AND DECIDED THAT GOLD LEAF HIGHLIGHTS WOULD BE STUNNING WITH THE SILVER.

RECIPE 27: HEADBOARD

Finish

Design with Gold Leaf

Time

Working time: about 5 hours
Total time (including drying): just under 2 days

At a Glance

1. Clean the headboard (10 minutes)
2. Apply base coat (20 minutes)
3. Let dry (2 hours)
4. Apply second base coat (20 minutes)
5. Let dry (2 hours)
6. Create design and pencil in (30 minutes minimum)
7. Apply design (about 3 hours)
8. Varnish (15 minutes)
9. Let dry (4 hours)
10. Apply second varnish coat (15 minutes)
11. Let dry (4 hours)

Materials

General

gloves, clean cotton rags, water, containers, stirrers, scissors

Preparation

flat latex paint—red clay
3" poly brush
low-tack masking tape

Designing

quick-drying gold size (water-base if you can find it)
approximately 3 books of composition leaf (Dutch metal)
#13 round acrylic brush
3" soft rabbit brush
#4 round acrylic brush
acrylic paints:
• black
• bright red
• bright yellow
• emerald green
• bright blue (ultramarine)
• white (to get pastels if you want them)

Varnishing

water-base varnish—satin
3" poly brush

Comments

• Since it's extremely unlikely you will have a headboard exactly like this one, feel free to make your own design. This is a "design and decoration" project as opposed to a "finish" project, so either copy me or go off on your own. *Any* headboard is going to make a major statement, so be sure your design will work (in terms of color and "feeling") with the piece itself and the rest of the bedroom.

STEP BY STEP

1 I masked off the silver border with low-tack masking tape and applied 2 coats of flat latex in a red clay color with a 3" poly brush, allowing each coat to dry for 2 hours.

2 This kind of design involves shapes, colors, and lines. Start as I did—by sketching ideas on paper.

3 When your design is finished, copy it onto the headboard with a pencil. Make the lines dark enough to see and don't worry about them—they will be covered either by gold leaf or by paint. Ask some questions. Want more of anything? Less? Is the design too symmetrical? Not symmetrical enough?

4 Use a #13 round acrylic brush and apply an even coat of gold size to the elliptical shapes. (It will be easiest to work with the headboard flat, rather than propped up in any way.) Start applying size from one side and work to the other. Gold size is an adhesive and the leaf won't stick anywhere without it. The reason I've specified an "even" coat is that if size sets up with ridges in it, they will be visible under the leaf. So apply the size carefully.

5 After you've finished applying gold size, wait a minimum of 15 minutes (2 hours if it isn't water-base). When the size has achieved the right "tack," your index finger will not glide easily over the surface, but neither will it stick. Now, leaf the elliptical shapes. Cut the binding (the selvage) on a book of leaf to free the individual sheets. (Have about 3 books of leaf on hand.) Pick up a leaf between its two pieces of rouge paper, let the bottom piece fall away, and place the leaf over the gold size. Press it down using your finger on the back of the rouge paper. Don't take the time to cut leaf to fit the shapes—just put on whole sheets. We will use almost all the excess

leaf (the "skewings") by the time we're finished. The natural oils in your hands will stain this gold leaf, so use the rouge paper whenever handling it.

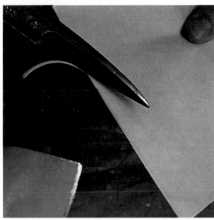

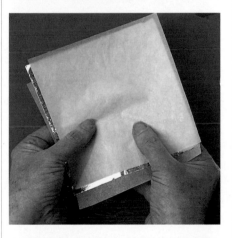

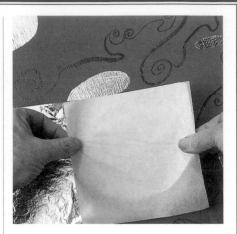

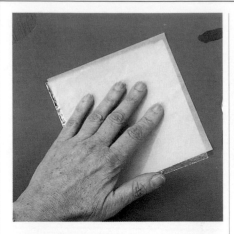

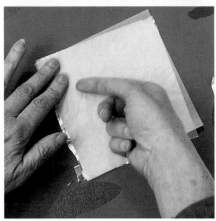

6 When you have applied leaf to all the elliptical shapes, use a 3" soft rabbit brush to "pounce" away the excess. Pick up skewings with your brush and work them into areas that you missed, then smooth the leaf with the same brush. As long as there is size on the surface, the skewings will stick there. When all the shapes have been smoothed, clean the skewings off the surface and place them in a separate box. Now use the rabbit brush or a rag to clean the surface because we're about to use gold size again.

7 Apply gold size to the lines and squiggles. Let the size set up for a minimum of 15 minutes (2 hours if not water-base) until it's the right "tack," then leaf the same way as before. When you're finished, place all the excess leaf in your skewings box.

8 The gold leaf alone might look wonderful—what do you think? If you want additional color, choose what looks best with your decor (or use the colors I chose). Use a #4 round acrylic brush and take color straight from the tube. (If you want pastels, mix color with white.) Paint inner circles in the elliptical shapes.

9 Now, *before* you varnish, take the headboard into the room it's going to live and prop it up on the bed. Does the design work? What about the colors, or lack of them? Are you satisfied? If not, now's the time to make adjustments.

10 Apply 2 coats of satin water-base varnish with a 3" poly brush. Let each coat dry for 4 hours.

11 Since the headboard will be so powerful a presence, you also might want to think about what goes with it. How about some new lampshades, sheets, bedcovers, curtains, and painted finishes on the wall.

DRESSING TABLE WITH MIRROR

● T'S NO ACCIDENT THAT THIS PROJECT IS THE LAST ONE IN THE BOOK—YOU CAN

CONSIDER IT YOUR GRADUATION EXERCISE. THIS PIECE TAKES THE LONGEST, IS

DAUNTING, DIFFICULT, TIME-CONSUMING—BUT *WORTH IT!* PLEASE DON'T TRY

THIS AS YOUR FIRST PROJECT, BUT AFTER YOU HAVE A FEW OF THE LONGER AND

MORE COMPLICATED ONES UNDER YOUR BELT, SET ASIDE THE TIME AND DO THIS

ONE. YOUR FEELING OF ACCOMPLISHMENT WILL BE IMMEASURABLE, AND THE BRAGGING

RIGHTS THAT COME WITH THE FINISHED PIECE ARE PRICELESS.

RECIPE 28: DRESSING TABLE WITH MIRROR

Finish
Blond Tortoiseshell with Ebony Inlay

Time
Working time: about 18¾ hours
Total time (including drying): about 13 days

At a Glance
1. Clean the table (15 minutes)
2. Shellac (30 minutes)
3. Let dry (30 minutes)
4. Apply base coat (30 minutes)
5. Let dry (24 hours)
6. Apply second base coat (30 minutes)
7. Let dry (24 hours)
8. Draw the design (1½ hours)
9. Tape alternating diamonds (1 hour)
10. Apply finish (4 hours)
11. Let dry (24 hours)
12. Varnish (30 minutes)
13. Let dry (24 hours)
14. Tape remaining diamonds (1 hour)
15. Apply finish (4 hours)
16. Let dry (24 hours)
17. Varnish (30 minutes)
18. Let dry (24 hours)
19. Apply ebony lines (1 hour)
20. Apply Polyshades (30 minutes)
21. Let dry (24 hours)
22. Apply second Polyshades coat (30 minutes)
23. Let dry (24 hours)
24. Varnish (30 minutes)
25. Let dry (24 hours)
26. Apply second varnish coat (30 minutes)
27. Let dry (24 hours)
28. Apply third varnish coat (30 minutes)
29. Let dry (48 hours)
30. Sand, polish, and buff (1 hour)

Materials
General
gloves, clean cotton rags, water, containers, stirrers, tack cloth
Preparation
masking tape and newspaper
alcohol

clear, white shellac
two 2″ poly brushes
satin oil-base paint—pale yellow
Finishing
pencil and ruler
painter's tape
single-edge razor blade (a new one), or crafts knife
artist oil—burnt umber
artist oil—raw sienna
artist oil—French yellow ocher
linseed oil
turpentine
Japan drier
mineral spirits
plastic teaspoons
#9 round bristle artist brush
2″ badger (or rabbit) brush
#6 round bristle artist brush
architect's tape—black, matte or shiny, ⅟₁₆″
Varnishing
oil-base varnish—gloss
Polyshades (by Minwax)—Honey Pine
2″ oxhair brush
a sheet of #600 wet/dry sandpaper
lemon oil
rotten stone
3 or 4 pieces of clean felt
spray wax (optional)

Comments and Tips
• I am breaking up this design into small sections because tortoiseshell finishes are very demanding. They take two characteristics that usually don't combine easily: being loose, free, and creative on one hand, and concentrating and being focused on the other. I suggest, therefore, that you work on the finish for a few hours and then stop. In addition, I'm varying the direction of the tortoiseshell within the diamonds to simplify the composition by providing contrast.
• Before any new shellac, paint, or varnish step, use a tack cloth to remove accumulated dust.

STEP BY STEP

1 If you can't remove the mirror, tape some newspaper on it for protection. Remove the hardware you can. (As your piece takes on its new life, you might want to consider replacing all this stuff.) Clean the table with alcohol and clean rags. Remove all the drawers to work on them separately.

2 Apply a coat of clear shellac with a 2″ poly brush and let dry for 30 minutes. Then apply 2 coats of pale yellow oil-base paint with another 2″ poly, letting each coat dry for 24 hours. Paint only the *visible* surfaces. I didn't paint the back of the piece because it's going against a wall.

3 After the second base coat is dry, pencil in the design. This is a critical step so take your time and do it precisely. As you can see, I have carried through the diamond motif on all the surfaces. On the wide, flat surfaces of the top and on the sides of the legs, I have done a "checkerboard" of diamonds, and on the narrower surfaces, I've done a strip of them.

4 Use the painter's tape to cover *every other* diamond. The idea is that no adjacent areas should be exposed. (This will enable us to tortoiseshell in the first direction, then come back in another step to tortoiseshell in the second.)

Note: Some people take very easily to taping geometric shapes like these, and others simply can't stand it. The only suggestion I can offer is to take your time, and if you're struggling, take frequent breaks. (Actually, best of all would be to bribe, blackmail, or cajole someone else into doing it for you.) This step has to be done precisely, so invest all the time you need to get it right. Also, you will find a sharp, *new* single-edge razor blade (or crafts knife) invaluable here.

5 On a palette, squeeze 2″ of burnt umber and next to it, 2″ of raw sienna. In a small container, make a glaze with 1 teaspoon of linseed oil, 1 teaspoon of turpentine, and 2 drops—only—of Japan drier. (The Japan drier will accelerate the drying time of the linseed oil.) Mix well.

Tip: Before you begin to apply this finish, hold out your hand, extend your fingers (including your thumb), and take a look. This is the shape of the tortoiseshell you're about to create. When you apply it, remember your fingers radiating upward and outward from your hand—or think of a fan. Keep either or both of these images in your mind as you proceed.

Note: Practice on a board before you approach your piece. There are two elements you want to feel comfortable with before you get too involved: the technique of *applying* the tortoiseshell, and the *color* (lighter or darker) of the individual diamonds.

6 Dip your #9 round bristle artist brush in the glaze, then pick up some burnt umber. "Mush" the brush around on your palette until the paint and glaze are mixed and the consistency is workable, then apply the color to your first diamond. Apply it in the "open hand" shape. Whisk with the 2″ badger or rabbit brush to soften the lines and remove the brush marks.

7 Do the same with the raw sienna, but avoid the areas where you applied burnt umber. Some glaze, some color, "mush" it around, and apply in the "open hand" shape. Whisk to soften and remove the brush lines.

8 Come back a second time with burnt umber to make the tortoiseshell darker. Use just a touch of glaze this time and decide as you're working just how dark you want the tortoiseshell to be. More or less burnt umber in this stage will control that choice. In this final step, whisk very gently.

Continue with the design in the *same* direction for all the uncovered diamonds. Take breaks when this begins to feel difficult. You have no deadline, so do not rush.

9 When you have completed all the exposed diamonds, remove the painter's tape and touch up any areas that need it with a clean rag and some mineral spirits.

10 After the paint has been allowed to dry for 24 hours, apply a coat of gloss oil-base varnish with a 2″ oxhair brush and let that dry for 24 hours.

11 When the varnish is dry, use painter's tape to cover all the diamonds you painted previously.

Note: The diamonds you are about to do will differ from the first set in two ways: We will apply them in a different direction, and we will make the color lighter. The tortoiseshell we first applied radiated upward and outward like your hand. These will radiate *toward* those diamonds from either side. A diamond on the left of a covered diamond will radiate from left to right, and a diamond on the right of a covered diamond will radiate from right to left. As to the lighter color, some French yellow ocher will take care of that.

12 Onto your palette, squeeze 2″ of burnt umber and next to it, 2″ of raw sienna, and next to that, 2″ of French yellow ocher. In a small container, make a glaze with 1 teaspoon of linseed oil, 1 teaspoon of turpentine, and (again) only 2 drops of Japan drier.

13 Dip your #9 brush in the glaze, and then pick up some of the burnt umber. "Mush" the brush around on your palette until the paint and glaze are mixed and the consistency is workable, and apply the color. If it's a diamond on the left of a covered diamond, radiate from left to right (and if it's on the right, radiate from right to left). Now whisk with the 2″ badger brush to soften the lines and remove the brush marks.

14 Use the #6 round bristle artist brush and do the same with the raw sienna, but avoid the areas where you applied burnt umber. Take some glaze, some color, "mush" it around, and whisk to soften and remove the brush lines.

15 With the same brush, do the same with the French yellow ocher and take a look. How light do you want the diamonds to be? More French yellow ocher will make them lighter; more raw sienna a little less light; and a mixture of raw sienna and burnt umber will darken them. Whatever you decide, gently whisk the last color you apply.

Note: You may find the lighter diamonds a bit less satisfying than the darker ones. But remember, they will work beautifully in the final finish as a *contrast* to the darker ones.

16 When you're finished, however, remove the painter's tape, clean up as needed, and let dry for 24 hours.

17 Apply a coat of varnish, and let that dry for 24 hours as well.

18 Apply the "ebony" lines using black ¹⁄₁₆″ architect's tape. The ebony lines will go in between all the diamonds to highlight their shape and enhance the contrasts of color and direction. The only caution here is that the tape cannot cross over one another, (because they form a bump) so be careful when you cut the intersections.

Tip: Don't press the tape down until you're sure of its position. The tape is very thin and will stretch if you put it down and take it up, so be sure before you press firmly. And just remember, however demanding you find this step to be, the alternative would be *painting* these lines (talk about demanding!).

19 When the ebony lines are firmly in place, apply a coat of Honey Pine Polyshades with a 2″ oxhair brush. This product combines stain and varnish. Let the Polyshades dry for 24 hours,

apply a second coat, and let that dry for 24 hours as well.

20 Apply 3 coats of varnish, letting each coat dry for 24 hours. After you have applied the third varnish coat, however, let it dry for 48 hours. We are about to do a sanding step and want to be sure the varnish has had enough time to dry. (In fact, if you live in a humid climate, let the table sit for one week.)

21 Now, moisten a piece of #600 wet/dry sandpaper and sand the piece smooth. Work slowly and carefully and have clean rags on hand to wipe off the residue as you work. What we are doing is actually cutting through the varnish to smooth it and even it off. This is why we needed 5 coats of protection. With any fewer, we would run the risk of sanding off the tape.

22 After the surface is smooth as the proverbial baby's bottom, make a paste of lemon oil and rotten stone (you want the consistency of toothpaste). Use a clean piece of felt and go over the entire piece with this mixture. Buff off the paste with a clean piece of felt as you go. This is a final sanding and polishing. After you're finished, either do a final buffing with another piece of clean felt or, if you want a shinier look, use spray wax. Remove the paper covering the mirror and install the new (or reinstall the old) drawer pulls.

23 You've spent some 13 days or so involved with this piece. *It* is gorgeous . . . and *you* have graduated. Congratulations!

SOURCE LIST

BENJAMIN MOORE & COMPANY
51 Chesnut Ridge Road
Montvale, NJ 07645
(800) 344-0400
Varnishes and paints

CHROMATIC PAINT CORPORATION
P.O. Box 690
Stony Point, NY 10980
(914) 947-3210
Japan paints

JANOVIC PLAZA
30-35 Thompson Avenue
Long Island City, NY 11101
(718) 786-4444
General paint supplies; catalog available

McCLOSKEY
1191 South Wheeling Road
Wheeling, IL 60090-5794
(800) 845-9061
Varnishes, glaze coat

PRATT & LAMBERT, INC.
P.O. Box 22
Buffalo, NY 14240
(716) 873-6000
Varnishes and paints

T. J. RONAN PAINT CORPORATION
749 East 135th Street
Bronx, NY 10454
(800) 247-6626
(718) 292-1100
Japan paints

PEARL PAINT COMPANY, INC.
308 Canal Street
New York, NY 10013
(800) 221-6845
(212) 431-7932
Paint and artist supplies

STENCIL WORLD CORPORATION
P. O. Box 1112
Newport, RI 02840
(401) 847-0870
All types of stencils

SEPP LEAF PRODUCTS
381 Park Avenue South
New York, NY 10016
(212) 683-2840
Leaf, size, bronze powders

S. B. ALBERTIS
322 West 57th Street
New York, NY 10019
(212) 247-0460
Saral paper

LIST OF OBJECTS

LIST OF TECHNIQUES

INDEX